Baseball's Greatest Players

The Story of John Ellis and the Fight Against Cancer

By James Herbert Smith

Enjoy!
James Herbert Smith

ELM GROVE

ELM GROVE

ISBN 978-1-940863-14-6

Library of Congress Control Number: 2021940558

Photo credit for cover: Connecticut Cancer Foundation
Left to right: John Ellis, Mickey Mantle, Whitey Ford, Billy Martin

Cover and book design: Ricketts-White Design

Dedication

For Reid MacCluggage, chairman of the board of Stars and Stripes, managing editor of The Hartford Courant and editor and publisher of The Day of New London. He showed me how to pursue what is true and how to write it so that people would want to know.

Also by the author

A Passion for Journalism/A Newspaper Editor Writes to His
Readers

Wah-say-lan/ A Tale of the Iroquois in the American Revolution

Wah-say-lan/ Seneca Warrior

A Boy's Life in the Baby Boom/ True Tales from Small Town
America

Opinionated Women in the Land of Steady Habits

Permissions

Thanks to:

Roger Angell for permission to quote from his 1984 New Yorker
essay "In the Fire."

The Associated Press and the Texas Rangers for photos of John
Ellis.

Topps Baseball Cards for the rookie All-Star cards of John Ellis and
Thurman Munson.

The Hartford Courant, The Day of New London and the Norwich
Bulletin for their photographs and their articles.

Also The New York Times, The New York Daily News, The Newark
Star-Ledger, The Christian Science Monitor, The Cleveland Plain
Dealer and Cleveland.com, The Dallas Morning News, The Connecti-
cut Post/HearstCT Media, author John Rosengren "Crossing the
White Line" in the History Channel Magazine; sports writer George
Popelka and the Cleveland sports website "Waiting for Next Year" for
their articles.

"I hope this goes on forever."

– Mickey Mantle
(quoted at first Celebrity Sports Banquet organized by John and Jane Ellis in 1988)

"Whoever wants to know the heart and mind of America had better learn baseball, the rules and realities of the game."

– Jacques Barzun

John Ellis signed with the Yankees when he was 17, just out of High School. In 1970, Topps Baseball Cards names him and his teammate, Thurman Munson, to its annual Rookie of the Year team. Ellis, called Moose at 6-foot, 2-inches carrying 225 pounds, played 13 years in the major leagues and was the first designated hitter in Cleveland Indians history. In his first year with the Texas Rangers he was batting .419 in 11 games when he slid into second base and broke his left leg and ankle. Out for the season. He came back to play 290 more games, batting .285 in 1979 with 61 RBI and 12 homers. Retiring from baseball, he went on to his fortune in real estate, only to be stopped by cancer that had also taken his older brother and sister. He pledged that, if he survived, he would help others. The Connecticut Cancer Foundation, founded by John and his wife Jane in 1987, has benefitted countless children and families struck by the disease. Every year, major league baseball superstars headline the foundation's annual fundraising dinner to carry on a generous tradition started by a kid who could swing a bat.

Table of Contents

Chapter 1 – A Promise..1

Chapter 2 – Bonus Baby...5

Chapter 3 – "Thunder" Ellis...11

Chapter 4 – Yankee Stadium...19

Chapter 5 – Who's on First?...26

Chapter 6 – Off to Cleveland...31

Chapter 7 – Cleveland Becomes Home.................................39

Chapter 8 – Ellis v. Robinson..47

Chapter 9 – A Texas Ranger...56

Chapter 10 – Superman Becomes Clark Kent.......................63

Chapter 11 – "I Understand End of Life Issues"..................69

Photos..72

Chapter 12 – Mickey, Whitey and Billy................................97

Chapter 13 – The Aflac Duck...102

Chapter 14 – Parade of Champions......................................107

Chapter 15 – Dining with the Stars......................................110

Chapter 16 – Ten Years In..115

Chapter 17 – Don Zimmer R.I.P. 122

Chapter 18 – "Welcome to our Mohegan homeland"..........126

Chapter 19 – "We will be the greatest charity"....................130

Chapter 20 – The Mission...136

Chapter 21 – The 2020 Dinner...141

Appendix

Foreword

John and Jane Ellis founded the Connecticut Cancer Foundation, which for more than three decades has committed millions of dollars to help families struck by the disease, and also has contributed generously to cancer research. This thoughtful thank you letter illustrates the sincere gratitude of the medical community.

Dear Jane Ellis,

"How far that little candle throws his beams! So shines a good deed in a weary world…" William Shakespeare ~ Merchant of Venice

Under your guidance, Bridgeport Hospital patients and families have generously benefited from financial assistance to meet their basic needs during a time when they are battling for life. I get the pleasure of hearing relief in patients and families voices and often seeing pleasure on their faces when learning that a (foundation) grant will pay their oil bill, keep their lights on, pay their rent and assist with much more. I often wonder if it is the gesture of knowing that people care and recognize their struggles or the actual cash assistance that makes them beam. I imagine it must be a combination. Thank you for keeping their hope alive and mine. I am empowered as a social worker when I have true practical ways to help our cancer survivors and their families.

Sincerely,

Philana Solomon

Oncology Social Worker

Norma F. Pfriem Cancer Institute Bridgeport Hospital

Chapter 1
A Promise

John Ellis was down but not out. Thirteen years a major leaguer, he never expected to be ripped open at Sloan Kettering Memorial Hospital. He was always tough, big, strong. He played baseball, like Lou Gehrig, with broken bones. He could hit the ball as long and as far as anyone in the game.

But the cancer was on its way to killing him, like it had killed his older brother and his sister. He was only 38, still a young man just three years out of baseball. He did not expect to live. The cancer was in his spleen and his chest. Hodgkins, third stage. They did the chest first.

They radiated his chest. John remembers thinking of Frankenstein. "There was a zapping noise," John imitates it: "mmmmmmmft – mmmmmmmft."

"They roast you," he says. "You look like a lobster. Red on the outside."

Even decades after, he chokes up talking about his older brother, "Richard, a teacher in New London. He was a year older than me. He was a serious, sensitive, nice person. He liked fly fishing. He liked the gentleness of life . . . he played basketball for St. Bernard's . . . his wife, Molly, died of breast cancer. It cost them $500,000 to fight the disease. They passed away in debt." John's sister, "Dolores, a housewife in Detroit . . ." John Ellis's voice trails off, she also died of breast cancer.

The youngest Ellis, Dave, got colon cancer, survived the operation only to contract leukemia. A first lieutenant in the Marines and then a career as a high school guidance counselor and licensed professional counselor, the father of three sons, survived.

Big brother John knew he was getting great care at Sloan Kettering, but he appealed to the Almighty. "I said to God 'you let me live, I'll help everybody I can'."

John Ellis meant that. But he thinks he is dying. He thinks his son and his daughter "won't get the benefit of my existence."

"I did not expect to live," John repeats. "I had my Jane with me. Jane believed. I didn't believe."

Jane not only believed, she also took seriously his pledge to help others. But first he needed to beat the cancer.

And he did. With his pledge to God, with Jane at his side, with expert medical care and with "My will to live." It is important to be "Helping others," he said. "You can be a survivor if you have a sense of humor and help others along the way. I understand end-of-life issues."

And they were planning something big. Something that people fighting cancer never expected. Something new for families struggling to survive against a deadly disease. The Connecticut

Cancer Foundation was a twinkle in John Ellis's bright blue eyes.

He would say years later about Memorial Sloan Kettering in Manhattan, that the man who attacked the cancer was a tough guy. "Achy was an Israeli tank commander."

"Medicine saved John's life. I was the messenger," the doctor said. "They called him the Moose. Absolutely, totally, his size and attitude helped John survive. Being the athlete he is and the man that he is. He's unique, determined, resourceful, ethical," said Joachim Yahalom, attending radiation oncologist at Memorial Sloan Kettering and professor of radiation oncology at Weill Cornell Medical College.

After John's recovery, Yahalom was treating another man "who was scared to death. He was shaken and that doesn't help. I called John. He came right down and met with this young man. John's enthusiasm, confidence got through. He later became a board member and raised funds for the foundation.

"I don't think John knew the foundation would become so big," Yahalom said.

From the beginning John and Jane were a team with great ideas. "Jane is complementary to John. She was with him since day one. She was with him every day through recovery," the doctor said.

"Jane has inspired me every day," said John. "What Jane does -- She's an angel on earth. What right do you have to live unless you help other people?" And then he underscored: "I never expected the foundation to be this big," but he came to expect it to be the greatest foundation in Connecticut.

He would recruit Mickey Mantle, Whitey Ford and Billy Martin to speak at the first celebrity dinner of their foundation. It raised $100,000. The Connecticut Cancer Foundation today has more than $10 million in assets and has given almost $9 million to benefit cancer patients, and for cancer research.

Chapter 2
Bonus Baby

John Ellis was 17 when he graduated from New London High School in 1966 in southeastern Connecticut, Boston Red Sox territory. But the New York Yankees' New England scout, Harry Hesse, was "very impressed with Ellis' desire, aggressiveness and power."

Hesse, "an old Eastern league first baseman of great repute," wrote one sports wag at the time, beat out several other scouts.

The Red Sox scout Bob Nicola "told me whatever the Yankees offer, we'll pay more," Ellis remembers with clarity, "But I really wanted to play for the Yankees."

Still, a whole lot of teams were after young Johnny Ellis. The scouts had gone to a game in Middletown to see a kid named Bobby Valentine, who wound up signing with the Dodgers. On the opposing Niantic team was John Ellis with a broken bone in his hand protected by a cast. But the kid saw an opportunity with all the scouts there, took off the cast and hit three home runs, one that soared over the Coginchaug River flowing behind the ball field. Down the left field line at Palmer field, that ball would have gone 450 feet. John's first homer in Yankee Stadium three years later traveled seven feet farther. Back when John was playing American Legion, Joe Rafferty was a busy guy. He was a retired police lieutenant, New London correspondent for The Hartford Courant, and a baseball scout for the San Francisco Giants.

"Mr. Rafferty came to me and said, 'John I'm taking you to meet the Giants brass and I think you'll be offered a contract.' I was afraid to tell him, but finally got up the nerve to say, 'Mr. Rafferty I'm sorry but I signed with the Yankees yesterday,'" Ellis told Hartford Courant Sports Editor Bill Lee.

John and his father drove down to Yankee Stadium that summer of '66 and signed a contract for a $10,000 annual salary with a $50,000 bonus – at 17. (The exact amount seems to be elusive and the Yankees say the records are gone. Two years later Thurman Munson signed with a $70,000 bonus).

The Yankees had the teenager do a little batting practice. Ellis stood at home plate at Yankee Stadium for the first time in his life and smacked one over the left field wall and into the stands.

"That's when the wall was out there," said former teammate Roy White. They moved the wall in since then.

Yankees manager Ralph Houk was nearly effusive when he said that day, "John is a youngster we have been watching for quite a while. A boy who swings a good bat and has lots of power."

Houk punctuated that observation with how his scouts "tell me he's as strong as an ox."

Ellis was born in New London Aug. 21, 1948 to Wanda and

Louis Ellis. His father was a Coast Guardsman and the family moved from Connecticut to Virginia to Michigan as Lou pursued the rank of chief petty officer. John was young and not yet an ox. But he was a three-sport athlete. Playing Pony League baseball in Mount Clemens, Michigan, the local newspaper reported that, "John Ellis took over in the fourth and pitched hitless ball while fanning seven."

He was Number One of the Top 20 Pony League batters, hitting .500 with four home runs.

He played jv basketball. In his team's 16th straight win he scored 22 points. And in football that year the local press crowed: "John Ellis throws 3 TD passes, runs for another in 31-0 romp."

In Michigan as a freshman on the varsity, "I threw 20 touchdown passes as quarterback, you don't really appreciate God's gifts. I probably did things I shouldn't have, like hit people too hard," John remembers. Earlier, in Little League, "I hit homers like you couldn't believe," he muses. His blue eyes widen. He sees himself doing it way back then.

He pauses, looks over, and says, he might not yet have been a big bruiser, but "I was a mean Little Leaguer. I was mean." Then he smiles. John Ellis has a near constant smile. "I played third base and the outfield, won a couple of state championships."

Back home in New London in the 1964 football season, after a growth spurt brought him up to 6' 2" and 205 pounds, "Ellis Outstanding as Whalers Trim Wilbur Cross 38-6" blared the headline. The New London High School fullback scored 22 points and "enjoyed his finest scholastic afternoon . . . it was all Ellis. The brilliant fullback caught the first Wilbur Cross punt . . . and rumbled 65 yards for the first score."

Game after game in the tough Capital District high school conference it went like this: "Ellis legged the ball for 29 yards to the 7-yard line." On the next play he "plunged from there for the score."

In the nation's oldest continuous high school football rivalry -- Norwich Academy v. New London High School began in 1875 -- The Norwich Bulletin's Brian Willett reported on the game in 1965. Ellis was "New London's near one-man show (who) did the kicking off, punting and called every offensive play, booted the extra point" in New London's 13-0 victory.

He won the Thames Trophy given annually in Groton/New London to the player who best typifies the qualities of sportsmanship, leadership and cooperation, and whose conduct and academic record has been satisfactory throughout the football season.

"He was one of the role models for us," said John's younger brother Dave. "We were both captains of the football and baseball teams, but he was a better athlete. He was a lot more aggressive than I was."

Dave Ellis went to UConn on a football scholarship and later made 1st Lieutenant in the Marine Corp, but his big brother "definitely was a tough guy. I used some of his tactics."

More than 30 colleges were offering the big brother football scholarships. The Green Bay Packers wrote to him urging he go for a college football scholarship. "It will not prevent you from playing baseball," the letter said, and "there are a great many advantages to a college football program" which could lead to "opportunities in professional football."

The spring of his senior year in 1966 John's baseball playing matched his moves on the gridiron. He drove in four runs with two singles and a home run against Hartford Public. In another game he hit two home runs. Against Fitch High of Groton, "Ellis smashed a three-run homer into the left field stands in the bottom of the eighth inning to give New London High a 4-3 victory." He was the first varsity player to hit a home run over the left field wall in Veterans Memorial Field in New London. Yogi Berra hit one out in 1945 when he was in the Navy at the submarine base.

In a 6-4 loss to New Britain High, there was a hint of things to come that didn't quite match the spirit of the Thames Trophy. He singled deep to left-center for an RBI but was thrown out trying to reach third base. Then he was ejected from the game for arguing the call.

In a game later that year against Fitch, John remembers that the opposing catcher, Paul Williams, was poised for John's slide into home plate. "He said something to me. Maybe I hit him too hard," John muses, pumping his big clenched fist into an opponent from half a century ago.

John was suspended from school for a week and kicked off the varsity team.

Back then, "we fought all the time," John says of his teenage years. One rival heard John was coming for him so he ran into a Friendly's restaurant and stayed there until it closed at midnight, avoiding a confrontation.

John went over to play American Legion baseball in nearby Niantic. One account has him hitting .465 for the season with six home runs, another has his batting average at an even .500. He made All State in football and was chosen for the baseball All Star team. Baseball was his future.

"Niantic may have the state's outstanding hitter in catcher-outfielder John Ellis," wrote The Courant's Pat Bolduc back then. He "seldom stepped out of the batter's box. He was always set to hit."

After John was signed by the Yankees, the New London City Council passed a resolution offered by Deputy Mayor Ernest F. Kydd Jr. John Ellis "has brought fame and glory to the city of New London ... therefore be it resolved said council hereby express its pleasure and pride" in the kid who was kicked off his high school team for a punch at the plate.

Years later John's daughter, Erika, would say with a sweet smile that her father was known as "the New London strong boy" for both his on-field and off-field demeanor.

Erika's brother, John Jr., remembered his father's tale of what he did when he signed with the Yankees. "He bought a brand new GTO (and two duplexes). He and a friend, Richie, went up to Maine hunting. They shot a bear. When they got back to New London they put it on the top of his car and drove around with it."

Chapter 3
"Thunder" Ellis

"We think John has a great future in baseball and as a Yankee," said Manager Ralph Houk in 1968. "He is aggressive, a hustler and a fighter."

"He hit eight home runs at Lauderdale at a ballpark in which the record is nine and which nearly always has a strong wind blowing from left field," said Public Relations Director Bob Fishel. "I saw him hit a grand slam home run there, which cleared the centerfield fence. I don't know of any other player ever hitting one over in that section of the park."

It was one of the longest homers ever in Fort Lauderdale, a 450-foot clout over the centerfield fence, noted the local press.

John Ellis "swings the most vicious bat in our organization," said Yankee Farm Director Johnny Johnston.

"Personally I like his temperament. We think it will be of great advantage to him. Ellis swings the bat real well and with a little experience behind the plate he may be ready to go sooner than many expect," said Houk.

Only one season out of high school in 1967 he batted .280 for Ft. Lauderdale in the Class A Florida State League, playing half the season before six months of National Guard duty.

He and Thurman Munson and many other professional athletes joined the National Guard. That same year Muhammad Ali was stripped of his world championship boxing title for refusing induction into the U.S. Army. Some 475,000 American troops were fighting in Vietnam.

Mini skirts were getting shorter, the Beatles came out with "Sgt. Peppers Lonely Hearts Club Band," the musical "Hair" debuted off Broadway and John Ellis was heading toward his second year with the New York Yankees organization.

In 1968, again for Single A Ft. Lauderdale, he was batting just .198. Manager Bill Shantz remained supportive. "I know John can hit, he'll come around," he said.

And he did. The press was crowing about "the young catcher's impressive finish." His totals for that season: 11 doubles, three triples and six homers.

At the end of August he was promoted to Triple A Syracuse where he came alive, hitting .432 in his first 37 at bats, including one home run that beat Buffalo on Aug. 30. Bison pitcher Bill Denehy had struck out 17, including three strikeouts by Ellis. When he came up in the 8th inning with a man on base, he swung, the ball sailed to left, hit the top of the wall and bounced over for his first Triple A homer.

John Ellis debuted in Triple A in a double header against the Mud Hens in Toledo. He had six hits including four straight in the nightcap, three of them reaching the left field fence.

"That boy certainly gets distance, even with broken bats,"

said Syracuse Manager Frank Verdi. John broke two bats that day.

It was 1968, the year Mickey Mantle retired with a lifetime .298 batting average and 536 homers. It was the year they lowered the pitching mound by 15 inches and the strike zone shrunk. It was harder to pitch, easier to hit. And it was the year John Ellis married his high school sweetheart, Angela DeLaura, at St. Joseph's Church in New London. Best man was John's brother Richard. His brother David was an usher. His sister Joan was a junior bridesmaid. The wedding announcement took note that the groom "is considered a prime prospect by the New York Yankees baseball team."

Their marriage lasted his entire baseball career and they had Erika and John Jr. before divorcing in 1986.

Ellis was hitting .348 for Syracuse at the end of the season and would be named to the New York Yankees 37-man roster for the 1969 season. He was 20 years old. Mantle would be a coach along with Dick Howser and Elston Howard. Houk was the manager. The other rookies were Ron Woods, 26, outfield; Dave McDonald, 26, first baseman; Jim Lyttle, 23, outfielder; Ron Kilmkowski, 25, pitcher; Bill Burbach, 21, pitcher; Ron Blomberg, 20, first baseman, outfield; and Thurman Munson, 22, catcher.

Only Blomberg (6 years,) and Munson (11 years) stayed for any length of time.

In the sometimes mysterious ways of professional baseball, John was back in Single A with the Kinston Eagles at the start of the season. On April 24 against the Raleigh-Durham Phillies he led his team from an eight-run deficit with six RBI to a 9-8 victory. He tied the game in the seventh inning with a three-run home run and then drove in the winning run with a single. He also singled home his team's first two runs. He was batting .358 with six homers and led the Carolina League with 28 RBI in 24 games.

Despite his success on that level, John admitted he was worried after two years in the minors.

"I've got a beautiful wife and a young baby to support now," he told one sports scribe. He was studying real estate at Mitchell College and contemplating a life of buying and selling rather than catching and hitting. Soon he was in Syracuse.

But the 20-year-old John Ellis looked ahead half a dozen years and lamented that if he were still in the minors, he'd quit the game.

A month later he was playing for the New York Yankees. Starting catcher Jake Gibbs was out with an injured index finger. Triple A Syracuse receiver Thurman Munson was doing National Guard duty.

"I'm going to keep you until Jake's finger gets better," Manager Houk told Ellis.

"I'm not going to let you send me down," Ellis retorted. Houk smiled.

On May 17, 1969 in an afternoon game with only 10,651 fans at Yankee Stadium John Ellis played his first major league game. It was against the California Angels.

"I didn't believe it until I heard the crowd roaring, just before the first pitch," he said at the time. "I still thought it was a dream. My arm was quivering."

Warming up starting pitcher Stan Bahnsen in the first inning

"I was so keyed up I threw the ball into centerfield when I threw to second" to start the game, said Ellis. When they played the national anthem "I had tears in my eyes. I didn't believe it was all happening."

He apologized later to Houk for the wild throw.

"My knees were shaking too, my first game," replied the manager, a catcher in his playing days.

Phil Pepe of the New York Daily News covered the game this way:

Johnny Ellis had the best seat in the house yesterday for the second major league game he has ever seen – right behind home plate. Johnny Ellis saw a terrific game . . . Johnny Ellis saw some pretty good Yankee hitting . . . He saw Bobby Murcer and learned why everybody has been talking about the Yankees' Young Reliable. Murcer lined a single and a double to stretch his hitting streak to seven games.

He saw Joe Pepitone snap out of his batting lethargy with a double and his ninth home run . . . Everybody else saw a kid named Johnny Ellis slam a 400-foot sacrifice fly and an inside the park home run that went 440 feet on the fly and rolled to the left-center field wall, 457 feet away.

The first major league game Johnny Ellis ever saw two years ago, was the day he signed his Yankee contract. The second one was yesterday. He played in that one.

As the outfielder hurled the ball from 457 feet, third base coach Dick Howser waved John home. The Newark Star Ledger's Jim Ogle wrote it this way:

The whole Yankee bench, including Houk, was up cheering the rookie on as he raced down the third base line gasping for breath. Gene Michael immediately pinned a nickname on the rookie, who is now known as Thunder Ellis.

The scoreboard flashed triple and error on the catcher. That started quite an uproar. But after viewing the play on tv, the scorer rightfully switched to an inside the park home run.

Forty-six years and one month earlier, another player hit his first home run in Yankee Stadium.

"I'd give a year of my life if I can hit a home run in the first game in this new park," Babe Ruth said. And he did, in the third inning of the opening day game April 18, 1923. The Babe died one week before John was born in August, 1948.
Pepe wasn't the only New York sage to notice the Yankee's big rookie:

By his 10th game this "hulking young man of 20" had 11 hits in 31 at bats for a .355 average, the highest on the club, noted George Vecsey of The New York Times. "All he does is attack the ball," including a line drive about 400 feet to the left-center fence for a double in his last at bat. When he's behind the plate, "He does not get rid of the ball quickly enough (and) has a bad habit of dropping his glove below the strike zone after catching low pitches . . . But he's learning."

In late June he was back for two weeks of National Guard duty in Connecticut. He had played in 15 games with the Yankees hitting .300 with five RBI and that one homer. And then he found himself back in Triple A Syracuse.

"When you stop and think of this kid, not yet 21, has only caught less than 80 games in his whole life and was catching for us in the big time this is quite a feat. John is high in our plans for the future," said Houk.

Ellis was back up June 8 for Mickey Mantle Day, catching Mel Stottlemyre in the opener of a double header, smacking a double. Mantle had retired after the 1968 season.

Introduced by "the voice of the Yankees" Mel Allen, the great Mick spoke to the sold-out crowd: "When I walked into this stadium 18 years ago I felt much the same way I do right now. I don't have words to describe how I felt then or how I feel now, but I'll tell you one thing, baseball was real good to me and playing 18 years in Yankee Stadium is the best thing that could ever happen to a ballplayer."

"I remember that day," says John Ellis. "I felt Mickey was uncomfortable."

It's a fellow ballplayer's sixth sense, something us just plain regular human beings can't tap into. It's an exclusive club, major leaguers knowing each other. Two decades later the Mick would be John's first speaker at his first foundation dinner to help cancer patients.

To John, back then, Stottlemyre "was an easy catch. He was in control and always knew what he was doing. If he was in trouble with men on the bases, he was more comfortable. He seemed to like that challenge and he would -- it seemed -- always get a double play to get out of it."

Maybe all major league catchers have it – an innate understanding of their pitchers.

Back in Syracuse the local press was headlining "Ellis on Hitting Binge."

"Ellis has been banging the ball at a lively clip ever since" being sent back down to Triple A. "Last night he hit for cycle – a single, double, triple and a homer, a grand slam his second in four days."

In 38 games he was hitting .333 with 41 hits in 123 at bats

with eight homers, eight doubles, three triples and 31 RBI. What the young ballplayer was saying to the Yankees was – don't you forget about me!

Houk was with some writers remembering an exhibition game in Orlando where John hit one over the centerfield fence where "you expect a Mickey Mantle or Harmon Killebrew to hit one," then offered up again John's nom de plume "Thunder."

However, the 21-year-old Ellis insisted he was not Thunder nor was he Harmon Killebrew. He was John Ellis, he said with some finality.

(For the record, Killebrew hit 573 homers in 22 years 1954-75 mostly with the Minnesota Twins).

Ellis was hitting balls out of the park. He earned rookie honors, hitting .368.

The Yankees announced "six outstanding minor league prospects will report to Yankee Stadium in September for the final month of the 1969 season," including two catchers: John Ellis and Thurman Munson.

On Sept. 18, 1969 Ellis beat Washington 4-3 on a 2-run pinch single. Munson was catching that day and went one for four. Mel Stottlemyre got his 19th win. Two days later Ellis was catching and went 2 for 3 against Baltimore. Munson caught and went 2 for 3 against Cleveland in the last game of the season.

Chapter 4
Yankee Stadium

Ralph Houk was holding forth to the local sporting press during spring training 1970.

"No matter where he plays, he gives you that added punch," he said of Johnny Ellis.

Maybe Houk was thinking of the time three years earlier when Ellis collided with teammate Gary Washington, who ended up with 10 stitches in his mouth. John merely brushed himself off. Or perhaps the Yankees' manager was recalling how earlier that spring Ellis and Charlie Sands collided at home plate. They both stood there a second, then the husky Sands fell to the ground -- out cold.

On March 21 that spring against the Los Angeles Dodgers, John played first base, hit in the cleanup spot and went 2 for 2, including a homer over the 401-foot sign in centerfield, to give the Yanks the victory.

"When Ellis is around, things seem to happen," said Houk. It was clear that Thurman Munson would be the Yankees' starting catcher. He was better at it, and he was hitting .355. But John was hitting .358 with four home runs, 18 RBI, 19 hits and he scored 11 runs.

"I started listening to people who knew more than I did and began studying smart pitchers. I learned the trick of going with the pitches, hitting the ball to right field and things like that," Ellis said at the time.

"I wanted to get both Ellis and Thurman Munson into my lineup and it was a lot more practical to move Johnny than to find another spot for Munson," Houk said. John quietly accepted his assignment. He made only one error that spring playing first base. And veteran first baseman Joe Pepitone, even though he led the team in home runs in 1969 with 27, was traded to Houston.

"It's incredible the way he has improved around the bag. When I first saw John I didn't think he had the hands to play ground balls, but he proved me wrong. He has already made great plays at first base, especially on ground balls, and he is getting better all the time," said Houk.

People were already comparing Ellis to another famed first baseman. "Yanks have another Skow," read one headline. "He could be the Yanks best right-handed hitter since Moose Skowron."

Decades later, Moose would be a featured attendee at one of Ellis' dinners to raise money for victims of cancer.

Ellis won the annual spring training James Dawson Award (an engraved wrist watch). Previous winners included Tony Kubek, Tom Tresh and Roy White.

"This year's Yankee hope of the future was going through

the motions of a first baseman. His name is John Ellis and in many ways he epitomizes these Yankees – young, enthusiastic, confident," wrote Phil Pepe of the New York Daily News. Yankees President Mike Burke "Talks about John Ellis in the special, reverent, respectful, hopeful tones reserved for Mr. Big," wrote Pepe.

"It goes back a year, this feeling Mike Burke has had about John Ellis . . . when the president took a liking to the young man. He gave him a present. A book."

"I had never done that before," Burke said, "But I felt he should read this book. It was Jerry Kramer's book. I thought it would be a good insight into how it feels to be in a major league. I was that sure that John would be here someday."

Never mind that Kramer's book was about the Green Bay Packers.

"Now John Ellis is not only here, but he's batting cleanup in today's opener," Pepe wrote.

As Ellis was dressing for the game, along comes a message from the woman who had been married to America's most memorable first baseman. Former Yankee president, 80-year-old Larry MacPhail, arrived carrying the slip of paper. He had tears in his eyes. He read the note out loud: "To John, For 30 years I have been looking for Lou's successor, if not better, and I am rooting for you. Eleanor Gehrig, Mrs. Lou."

The boy was really impressed and so were the rest of us," Manager Ralph Houk told the Christian Science Monitor.

Said Ellis: "I only hope that I can live up to her expectations. It's a tall order . . . . I don't think there will ever be another Lou Gehrig . . . He was quite a man. He played when he was hurt and he was a leader who always gave 100 percent. That's the type of guy I want to be."

One scribe wrote that he put the note "carefully in his locker." Another reported he gave the letter to a writer "for safe keeping." Her note is not in Ellis' voluminous scrapbook put together by his father and John couldn't recall 49 years later where it was.

Ed Rumill, the chief sports columnist for The Christian Science Monitor, wrote, "Ralph Houk's 1970 edition of the New York Yankees, which has a much improved look in the Eastern Division of the American League, showed a strapping rookie at first base . . .

"The boy's name is Johnny Ellis and at 6 ft, 2 in, and 220 pounds he is built the way you expect Yankee first sackers to be built," wrote Rumill.

Before that first game of the 1970 season Houk said John is "amazing" at first base and "it's a joy to watch him swing a bat."

The New York Daily News' season-opener photo spread put it this way: "In his soph season, Johnny Ellis could be a big surprise. The most physically powerful (6'2" and 220 pounds) of the new Yanks, Ellis is the most likely candidate to start belting the tape-measure homers that used to be a Bomber trademark."

The opening game was Yankees v. Red Sox. Out on the field in the second inning the 21-year-old first baseman acted like a veteran. He walked over to visit Mel Stottlemyre on the mound after the Red Sox got their first run.

"Don't worry, we'll get that back," John told Mel.

Ellis scored the Yankees' first run of the year after being hit by a pitch. In his last at bat he sizzled a single past shortstop Rico Petrocelli and got the only hit off reliever Bill Lee.

As the season began, "He really has box office magnetism. Ellis has a chance to be the best-liked Yankee in history," quipped Mike Burke.

He lead a Yankee sweep of the Indians, 6-5 and 8-1, hitting a homer in each game of a double header.

In Minneapolis he homered in the third inning and snapped a 6-6 tie in the fifth with a double. In Detroit he blasted "a nearly cloud-high three-run homer."

In the end, the Yankees took second place with 93 wins and 69 losses. Ellis, the youngest player on the team, played in 78 games, hit .248 with 29 RBI, 12 doubles, one triple and seven home runs in 226 at bats.

"John did a real fine job for," said Houk, who was named the American League Manager of the Year.

But all was not well in this 1970 season. Thurman Munson started out 1 for 30. Ellis went a similarly paltry 4 for 44 early in the season.

"It has been a long way back," Ellis said at the end of the season. "Houk noticed there was something wrong with my stance and that helped me get out of the slump."

Munson was named Rookie of the Year, hitting .302 in 132 games with 53 RBI, 25 doubles, four triples and six home runs. Ellis had acknowledged to himself that Munson was the better catcher and now he knew the guy was terrific at bat too. They would become more than teammates.

It turned out that Ellis at first base and Munson behind the plate made the 12th annual Topps baseball card Rookie All-Star team along with Bernie Carbo of the Cincinnati Reds, Larry Bowa of the Philadelphia Phillies, Billy Conigliaro of the Red Sox, Roy Foster of the Cleveland Indians, among others.

Major league players voted for the rookie all stars. "This should be a real source of pride," wrote Topps Chewing Gum Sports Director Sy Berger to their rookies of the year. "Our most sincere congratulations and best wishes for continued success in baseball."

Ellis and Munson "were very close friends," said Joe Stellato decades later, gazing at framed photos of both players in his Waterford, Conn. condo. Stellato, a bank president, was the first president of the foundation.

"They had a very good relationship. And they had a pact. When John was traded to Cleveland where he would be their starting catcher, he and Thurman agreed, if one of them was on base and coming home attempting to score" there wouldn't be any violent collisions. "He and John shook hands on that. Thurman didn't play the game lightly, neither of them did," said Stellato, but these two catchers had a friendship pact.

Years later in Texas when John was playing for the Rangers against the Yankees, "He was heading home but he was a dead duck. Thurman had the ball and John was three or four feet away. He stopped, Thurman stood up, they patted each other."

John Ellis knew he was out and he kept his pledge to his friend. In August, 1979 he joined all of Munson's Yankee teammates and took the day off to go to the Yankee captain's funeral. Joining John from the Rangers were Mickey Rivers, Sparky Lyle, Dave Rajsich and Doc Medich.

Forty years later Ellis looked back and said of Munson: "He had grit. He had heart, but you have to have grit. He had both."

Chapter 5
Who's on First?

It must have felt like a merry-go-round, or maybe a roller coaster, for young John Ellis. Joe Pepitone was gone and the Yankees brought in veteran first baseman Danny Cater from Oakland. He ended up hitting .301 in 155 games as the Yankees' regular first baseman.

Houk tried Ellis out at third base.

"I want to become a regular and I think I can make it at third if that is where Ralph wants me," Ellis told a sports writer. "I think I can play acceptably. Not great, but good enough. I had no trouble with my throwing and I felt comfortable," the strapping sophomore said.

In winter ball in Puerto Rico he played 20 games at third. As the 1971 season began Houk said, "Because of his big bat . . . John will be in there somewhere."

Said Ellis: "My aim is to crack the regular lineup." He didn't know where, but, "I'm going to be in there."

"I'd better find a spot for him. He's big, tough and unhappy when he isn't playing," Houk told The Hartford Courant's Bill Lee. "John made himself a Yankee last year. I've never managed a player more competitive or who worked harder than John Ellis."

He is big and tough but, "I cried when they put me on third base. I didn't know how to play ground balls," he admitted to Lee who went on to write, "The powerful man from New London is looked upon as having more long ball potential than anybody else on the team." Lee had been covering sports for nearly 50 years at the time.

Another veteran sportswriter Joe Trimble of The New York Daily News weighed in: "Houk has to find a position for 22-year-old Johnny Ellis, either at third or first base. The 225-pounder could be the most exciting Yankee since Mantle."

Comparisons inevitably came up: "If the Twins were able to win pennants with Harmon Killibrew at third, then the Yankees feel that their kid – who has the size of a linebacker – won't be a liability at that position," wrote Trimble.

The Yankees were trying to make sure of that. Former Yankees third baseman and minor league manager Bobby Cox was hitting a hundred ground balls a day at Ellis. When Cox wore out, coaches Dick Howser or Elston Howard took over.

"Then he goes out in right field and does 100 pushups and back bends," said Howard.

Said Cox, "Johnny is rather light and quick on his feet for such a big man. He handles ground balls well. We haven't worked on bunts yet. He has to learn to come in on the ball and make the off balance throw."

John must have been puzzled. He found himself behind the plate in a spring training game against Detroit. Puzzled but proficient. He hit a 450-foot homer, two doubles and scored three runs. Dick McAuliffe tried to score, but met Ellis at the plate. McAuliffe, a 175-pound infielder, was carried off the field on a stretcher.

As spring training wore on and John kept making errors at third base he mused aloud that, "being platooned is the farthest thing from my mind and Ralph and I have had words about it . . . but I could be in a lot worse places than I am now."

He was playing first base in the second game of a doubleheader in Cleveland May 23. With the game tied 1-1 in the eighth inning, Cleveland starter Sam McDowell slid hard into second base trying to prevent a double play. He and Yankees shortstop Gene Michael wound up wrestling each other to the ground. Both benches emptied, including managers and coaches, and the battle was on.

Ellis was pummeling McDowell before they were buried under a pile of teammates. When Ellis came out he was swinging at everyone wearing a Cleveland uniform. He nor anyone else was ejected.

The consensus was that Ellis won the fight, but the Indians won the game 2-1 in McDowell's first complete game of the season.

Ellis refused to talk about it except that it was his first major league fight. "It was just one of those things," he said.

Decades later he would remember: "Sudden Sam McDowell. I hit the guy with everything I've got. I was going to make sure he never pitches again. The next night he throws a one-hitter. Shows how tough I was."

But back then, it wouldn't be the last time John Ellis found himself brawling on the baseball diamond.

"How many fights in your career John?"

"I couldn't tell you. In Kansas City once, I was with Texas. Pitcher Eddie Farmer threw 98 mph but he never knows where it's going. He breaks Al Cowan's jaw. Next up Frank White. Breaks his hand. A fight breaks out. There's fighting everywhere. The president of the American League Lee MacPhail ordered a $10,000 fine if I leave the bench."

Looking back on John's baseball career, Hartford Courant sports columnist Bob Sudyk put it this way: "Every professional sport has its enforcers, and Ellis ranks among the best in baseball. He was a walking peace treaty in the midst of bean ball wars and bench-clearing brawls. Yankees Manager Billy Martin, connoisseur of combat, said, 'Johnny Ellis was a hard-nosed player who gave up his body for his teammates. Anybody messing with someone on his team automatically was messing with Johnny. He was the one you looked for when trouble started, an intensely loyal teammate'."

Two days before the McDowell dustup, the story on John was that he hit a homer off Oakland's Catfish Hunter at Yankee Stadium.

"The lone alien in Ralph Houk's left handed-hitting lineup, the muscular first baseman poled a three-run homer to provide Fritz Peterson's cushion in a 5-3 Yankee triumph . . . Ellis, whose pre-game .341 average earned him one of his rare starts against a right-handed pitcher, turned a 2-2 knot into the Yankees third straight victory with his No. 3 homer in the fifth. The drive . . . followed a three-bagger by Roy White," wrote Red Foley of the New York Daily News.

Oakland's "hard-throwing right-hander" Blue Moon Odom won the second game holding the Yankees to six hits, including a double by Ellis.

The week before his 23rd birthday John faced Oakland's Vida Blue who would win 24 games in 1971 and strike out 301. Ellis pinch-hit a double into left-center to tie the game before 45,343 fans in Yankee Stadium. Pitchers were still batting then and Blue went 2 for 3 (Reggie Jackson went 2 for 5) in the 6-4 Athletics victory. It wasn't a great 23rd birthday Aug. 21 in Anaheim as John, pinch-hitting, hit the ball but not safely, going 0 for 1 in an Angels 2-1 victory. The Yanks had only six hits that day.

Chapter 6
Off to Cleveland

In 1971, his third year with the Yankees, John played in 83 of 162 games, went to the plate 238 times with 58 hits, 34 RBI, three home runs and a .244 batting average.

He wasn't happy with his part-time status.

"I want to be traded," he told his hometown press. "I want to go somewhere where I can play. I'm just not too happy."

Yankee Stadium "is hard for a right handed hitter. I know I can do better elsewhere." He mused, "I think they know I could hit better for another team and that's why they haven't traded me." Then he added, "I think they might trade me if they get the right offer."

A week before the 1972 season opened, 23-year-old John Ellis went to 53-year old Manager Ralph Houk and told him he felt his career wasn't going anywhere and that "I was getting stagnant."

The Major, as Houk was called, like Ellis, was a star high

school athlete signed by the Yankees as a catcher in 1939. But World War II was coming. After three years playing in the minor leagues, Houk enlisted in the Army as a private. After officer candidate school, he was promoted to lieutenant. He fought at Normandy and the Battle of the Bulge in 1944, receiving a Silver Star and eventual promotion to major.

In his first game with the Yankees in 1947, Houk got three hits, batting .272 in 41 games. But then there was Yogi Berra, and Ralph Houk became the bullpen catcher.

The "stagnant" Ellis in 1972 said Houk "told me to be patient . . . that I'm still learning . . . that I'm the type of player he wants and that by next year something should work out."

And so the season began, the headlines shouted:

***John Ellis Delivers Key Hit
As Yankees Sweep Rangers***

***Ellis Helps NY
Beat Tigers Twice***

***Three Run Homer for Ellis
Over Left Field Wall At Fenway***

In the annual Mayor's Trophy Game in August the headline read: "Yanks Edge Mets 2-1 on Ellis Homer." As they say, you can look it up. There were 52,302 eyewitnesses at the game and The Ultimate Mets Database puts it this way: "Met manager Yogi Berra opted to replace (pitcher Brent) Strom with Bob Rauch in the sixth. But this use of managerial strategy backfired, for batter John Ellis promptly knocked the ball out of the park to put the Yanks ahead and cap the scoring for the evening."

Three weeks later under the headline "Yanks Sweep Tribe" the New York Daily News' Phil Pepe wrote, "There's life in the Yankees yet. John Ellis, Rob Gardner and Sparky Lyle did a little artificial respiration to keep the heart thumping . . . Ellis was the hitting hero of the second game, with a double and two singles, three RBI to raise his batting average to .300."

On Sept. 24 Ellis caught the second game of a double header and had two singles, a double, three RBI leading the 8-2 Yankee victory.

But the Yanks were in third place after a September collapse.

"The fans in southeastern Connecticut are discouraged with Manager Ralph Houk and his handling of John Ellis," wrote Bob Nauta of The Day of New London. "It is difficult to understand how Houk can leave Ellis on the bench. Ellis is a power hitter and the Yankees certainly could have used some hitting in the past four weeks. But Houk went with his regular line up and Ellis sat on the bench for the most part."

John played in only 52 games, 30 fewer than the year before. But he hit an enviable .294 with five home runs and five doubles in 136 at bats.

Looking back on his stint with the New York Yankees, a philosophical John Ellis says today, "I was 20 and batting fourth for the New York Yankees in 1970! I wasn't ready to bat 4th for the New York Yankees."

The 70-year-old Ellis caught himself a few moments later:

"I was a pro. I could hit, catch at a major league level." And the Cleveland Indians thought so.

He was playing winter ball in Puerto Rico when it came out that he was being traded to the Indians for Graig Nettles. The Dec. 4, 1972 letter from the Yankees said, "Dear John, Herewith enclosed is official player transfer notice number 2996 advising you that your contract has been assigned outright from the New York Yankees to the Cleveland Indians Baseball Club. Kindest regards to you and your family," Lee Mac Phail, General Manager.

Mac Phail penned a side note on the official stationery, "John, I want to talk to you. May try to call you in P.R. or will see you when you return." L.M.

But the team John was playing for in Mayaguez went bankrupt and folded. He was back in New York when he heard the news of his trade on the radio. Then "I saw my name in the paper and realized the news was official."

Many of the Yankees sent each other Christmas cards and when Ralph Houk's arrived it said, "Thanks John for all your effort you gave me. I wish you the best of luck with your new team. I will miss you."

John hit .260 in 235 games over four years for the Yankees. He had 172 hits, 9 RBI, scored 55 runs and hit 16 homers. He didn't think he had "that much of a chance" with the Yankees with only 662 at bats and 580 in the Yankees farm system.

At the time Ellis pointed out two memorable days in his career, one involving the Indians. He went 5 for 8 including two doubles, two home runs and five RBI in a double header against Cleveland in 1970. The other was the year before with

Syracuse when he was called up, had to fly all night to California and caught Stan Bahnsen's two-hit shutout over the Angels.
The trade was a multi-player deal. Along with Nettles, the Yankees got reserve catcher Gary Moses. Besides Ellis, Cleveland
got third baseman Jerry Kenney and outfielders Rusty Torres
and Charley Spikes.

"We traded tomorrow for today," quipped Mac Phail.

Nettles was the "Indians Man of the Year" in 1971 when he
led Cleveland in seven offensive categories.

"You hate to give up the guys we did," said Houk, "but
there aren't many Nettles around either."

Hartford Courant Sports Editor Bill Lee put it this way:
"Ellis' status hasn't improved that much in the Cleveland camp
because (the Indians') Ray Fosse is one of the best catchers in
baseball and nobody figures to move Chris Chambliss off first
base."

But as the news sank in, John began leading with his chin.
"That stadium in New York hurt me. Too much room in left
center field," he told Lee. "I thought I was strong enough to
beat it, but I wasn't. I am sure the Cleveland park will be better
for me."

The new designated hitter slot would be fine with him. He
wanted to bat 400 times in a season, something he had never
done.

First base or catch, didn't matter to him. "It's all the same to
me. You have to be able to move around, shift your feet a lot at
both positions. And someone is always throwing the ball at
you," he said.

John was 24, beginning his seventh year in professional

baseball, his fifth as a major leaguer. He was hitting .296 that spring for Cleveland and doing most of the catching. And then Fosse was traded to Oakland.

Fosse "would not have been traded if Ellis had not impressed some people this spring," said Indians public relations man Dino Lucarelli.

John is still smiling when he thinks of the April 9, 1973 game in New York.

The headline was "Ellis helps Tribe Stop Yanks 3 to 1"

"Run-scoring hits by ex-Yankees Rusty Torres and John Ellis helped the Cleveland Indians to a 3-1 victory Monday that spoiled New York's home opener."

A month later The Cleveland Plain Dealer's Russell Schneider covering Indians v. Oakland, described "the best play of the game from the Indian's standpoint, was the way John Ellis blocked the plate on Deron Johnson in the second inning of the nightcap. Johnson tried to score from second on Gene Tenace's single to left. Walter Williams' throw was on target, though high, and as Ellis went up for the ball, he also blocked Johnson.

"They went down in a heap and Ellis, kicked in the chest, had the wind knocked out of him. But the hard-nosed catcher applied the tag and held onto the ball."

Ah, the play at the plate. The New Yorker's Roger Angell described it best in his 1984 essay "In the Fire."

Consider the catcher. Bulky, thought-burdened, unclean, he retrieves his cap and mask from the ground (where he has flung them, moments ago, in mid-crisis) and moves slowly again to his workplace. . . Armored, he sinks into his squat, punches his mitt, and becomes wary, balanced, and ominous; his bare right hand rests casually on his thigh while he regards, through the portcullis, the field and deployed fielders, the batter, the base runner, his pitcher, and the state of the world, which he now, for a waiting instant, holds in sway. The hand dips between his thighs, semaphoring a plan . . .

These motions—or most of them anyway—are repeated a hundred and forty or a hundred and fifty times by each of the catchers in the course of a single game, and are the most familiar and the least noticed gestures in the myriad patterns of baseball. The catcher . . . must be large, brave, intelligent, alert, stolid, foresighted, resilient, fatherly, quick, efficient, intuitive, and impregnable . . . Most of all, the catcher is invisible. He does more things and (except for the batter) more difficult things than anyone else on the field, yet our eyes and our full attention rest upon him only at the moment when he must stand alone, upright and unmoving, on the third-base side of home and prepare to deal simultaneously with the urgently flung or incoming peg and the onthundering base runner—to handle the one with delicate precision and then, at once, the other violently and stubbornly, at whatever risk to himself.

"I guess that blocking the plate is the one thing I know how to do well," said Ellis after the game.

"It was fantastic," said Indians Manager Ken Aspromonte, "Usually when a catcher has to jump for the throw he gives up the plate to the runner. But John didn't. It was a heck of a play."

And there was 6' 2" 210-pound John the base runner. In the photos this same season in a May 20 double header against the Yankees, you can see Graig Nettles jumping high as Big John starts his slide into third base. He's called safe, but his momentum carries him past the bag. Now Nettles is on his hands and knees at the bag and tags Ellis as he scrambles back. "Out," called the umpire.

Chapter 7
Cleveland Becomes Home

John Ellis played in only 52 games with 40 hits his last year as a Yankee. He will play in 127 games with 118 hits as an Indian in 1973. It was as if Cleveland put out its welcoming mat:

"Ellis Earns Tribe Split" with a 9th inning single "that carried the Cleveland Indians to a 6-5 victory over the Chicago White Sox." . . . "Ellis Paces Cleveland," against the Texas Rangers with a home run. "Tribe Topples Tigers 8 to 7" with Ellis' 8th inning homer . . . "John Ellis' windblown three-run homer into the left field screen in the 4th inning powered the Indians to a 4-2 victory. He went one for three in the first game as the designated hitter and three for five in the second as Cleveland's catcher . . ." "John Ellis' Six RBI Help Power Indians to Win Over Boston."

"The Red Sox tried to draft him out of high school. They should have . . . "Indians Edge Bosox 1-0 on HR by Ellis." "John Ellis cracked a second inning home run to back the 5-hit pitching of Gaylord Perry and carry the Cleveland Indians to a 1-0 victory over the Boston Red Sox Wednesday. Ellis led off the second with his 14th homer over the left field fence off Bill Lee."

He was getting good press. The Cleveland Plain Dealer called him "the vastly under rated catcher/first baseman."

Cleveland Press Sports Editor Bob August wrote that "Ellis is getting his opportunity to prove he is the hitter he thought he could be and he is getting the chance in a ballpark tailored to his dimensions."

He quoted John, "Everyday I go to the stadium with the feeling that anything can happen, that I could have a really great day. It's an entirely different feeling, something I never had at Yankee Stadium."

Under the headline: "Would You Believe a Happy Indian," August wrote that John "is a notoriously hard loser on a team that has been absolutely uncanny in finding ways to lose. When frustrated, Ellis has a temper that sometimes erupts like Old Faithful and he is inclined to throw things around, sometimes the things being other ball players." As we shall see.

His first year in Cleveland he was welcomed with open arms. In mid-June the Plain Dealer trumpeted "Ex-Yankee Ellis Is Hero Again" explaining how sports scribes didn't have to work too hard to select the most valuable player of the game, each home game.

"Decisions had to be made on Sunday night and again on Tuesday, however both times the vote went to John Ellis, the husky fugitive from the Yankee organization."

John Ellis was an Indian. He was soaring, his team was not.

They finished in last place in 1973 with 71 wins and 91 losses under Manager Ken Aspromonte who had played with six teams in seven years. 1974 would be his third as manager of the Indians. He wrote to his players Jan. 28 that year:

"I am looking forward to a winning season . . . in which you and your teammates make significant progress toward greatness." He told them if they "improve 10 percent the Cleveland Indians will be the talk of the baseball world."

As the season began, Ellis declared that "I deserve the chance" to be the Indians' starting catcher. But in a double header against the Yankees, they stole half a dozen bases with John behind the plate.

At bat it was a different story. In a game against the Red Sox, John and his teammate Chris Chambliss each hit safely, extending their hitting streaks to 12 games each. And then on May 13 "Ellis' 3-run homer lifts Tribe past Red Sox" blared the headline on the story that began: "There's no place like a virtual tie for first place. The Indians made it to that lofty platform Monday night with a rousing 4-1 victory over the Boston Red Sox." Ellis's homer came in the first inning against Luis Tiant. Red Sox announcer Ken Coleman dubbed Ellis the Moose.

Perhaps that was after the first time John met Don Zimmer, "who was known as Popeye the fighting Sailor Man," John recalled. "Zim was a players' manager I was convinced of this because I was playing 1st base for Cleveland at the time and Zim was coaching 3rd base for Boston. A brawl breaks out and on the bottom of the pile is Zim fighting and wailing with his arms and I have him in a headlock. 'Zim what are you

41

doing????' I asked."

Then the umps broke up the fisticuffs.

At the end of the month, May 29, there was a game in Texas where the Rangers beat the Indians 3-0, but not before John got in a punch or two. The Rangers' Lenny Randle laid down a bunt, ran down the first baseline and threw an elbow at Cleveland pitcher Milt Wilcox. Ellis was playing first base, ran and tackled Randle. Both benches emptied. Texas Manager Billy Martin charged into the fray and was knocked on the seat of his pants. Then it was over. No one was ejected.

"John Ellis was the toughest badass who ever played for the Cleveland Indians," wrote George Popelka in 2014 on the Cleveland sports website "Waiting for Next Year."

"Sure, the franchise has had its full share of hot heads, and guys who weren't afraid to fight. None of them fought as often and won as thoroughly as Ellis. Ellis' personality was reserved most of the time, but when it was time to fight, he was said to have 'that look'," according to Popelka.

A look from John could also defuse a situation. In a game against the Red Sox in Boston, Cleveland pitcher Bill Burbach threw a wild pitch into George "Boomer" Scott's back. Boomer was a talented and intimidating power hitter who trotted to first base, staring and grumbling at Burbach. When he got to first base Ellis was waiting and said something to George, who then simmered down, noted teammate Fritz Peterson, who had taken out a $1 million insurance policy in case he got pulled into a fight sparked by John.

Roy White, John's Yankees teammate, remembered that, "John wouldn't back off if challenged. He wouldn't take anything from anybody. He was a good guy to have on your team."

Sometimes it was off the field. John remembers enjoying the company of New York Daily News writer Phil Pepe in a New York bar.

"Some guy comes over and starts bad-mouthing Phil. Suddenly he punches me in the mouth. Splits my lip. 'You motherfucker! I yell.' I beat the shit out of the guy. Got a couple of stitches. Played the next day," said John.

There would be more fisticuffs before John Ellis hung up his spikes. Too bad he was out with an injury when Texas was in Cleveland June 4. The official Major League Baseball Reference web site puts it this way:

Tuesday, June 4, 1974
Attendance: 25,134
Venue: Cleveland Stadium
Game Duration: 3:05
Night Game, on grass
Game was forfeited to the visiting team. Ten-cent beer night went horribly awry as drunken Cleveland fans attacked Texas outfielder Jeff Burroughs and the umpires.
Umpires declared a forfeit win by Texas over Cleveland.

The game is part of baseball lore. One headline 35 years later:

"Cleveland Indians' Ten Cent Beer Night: The Worst Idea Ever"

Eight-ounce Stroh's beer for a dime induced one woman to run onto the Indians on deck circle flashing her breasts and trying to kiss the umpire. A naked man ran onto the field and slid into second base. Two guys ran onto the field and mooned the fans.

Thinking one of his players had been attacked, Texas Manager Billy Martin Hollered, "Let's go get 'em boys!" grabbed a fungo bat and the Rangers followed.

Aspromonte told his players to grab bats and defend the Rangers against the inebriated Cleveland fans. Joe Tait and Herb Score calling the game on radio, noted the lack of police. A riot squad appeared and ended the brawl.

The game was forfeited in favor of Texas, which had a man on second when the melee erupted.

After that, fans were limited to four beers a night.

It was only three days earlier June 1, 1974 at home against the Kansas City Royals, when John reached for a wide throw, left the bag, caught the ball then kicked back to touch the base. The Royals' Hal MacRae was digging out a grounder when Ellis's foot hit MacRae's knee and both players crumpled to the ground.

"I just couldn't get up," Ellis said at the time. "I thought it was a muscle pull. Then there was a rain delay and by the 9th inning I couldn't even move."

John, the first designated hitter in Cleveland's history, with a team high 25 RBI, had broken his ankle bone and was out of action for a month. His foot was in a cast, but every morning at 10:30 he reported to a portable batting cage under the center-field bleachers and then moved into exercises to keep his throwing arm in shape.

On July 1 with 29,801 fans in Cleveland Stadium for a double header against Milwaukee, John came off the disabled list. He singled twice and scored once as DH in the first game.

Catching the second game he slammed a 3-run homer in the first inning and singled in two more runs in the 5th. He was 4 for 8 with 5 RBI.

"John Ellis Returns With a Bang," blared one headline.

"There was never any doubt about Ellis having a job back . . . He came on strongly enough to return instantly to the start status he held before the injury," wrote one Cleveland scribe.

"Ellis Earns a New Label: He's the Tribe's Mr. Clutch" rang the headline over Russell Schneider's Plain Dealer article.

"Cleveland – Who's the best clutch hitter in the America League?

"As far as I'm concerned, John Ellis is," said Indians Manager Ken Aspromonte, "I'd rather have John up there when we really need a run than anybody else.

"The 26-year-old slugger came from the Yankees two years ago in one of the Indians best-ever trades. In 127 games last season Ellis batted .270 including 14 homers and 68 RBI. This year he's even better, despite losing four weeks with a broken bone in his right foot. Ellis was batting .285 with 8 homers and 43 RBI after the Indians' 100th game.

"Most of all I admire John because he gives 100 percent all the time . . . he always plays to win and that's why I want him in the lineup everyday." Aspromonte said.

Ellis caught Dick Bosman's no-hitter at home on July 19 against the Oakland Athletics as 24,302 fans watched Bert Campaneris, Sal Bando, Reggie Jackson, Claudell Washington, et al never reach first base.

The next day The Hartford Courant headline trumpeted: John Ellis Powers Tribe to 10-9 Victory over A's

He drove in five runs – two with a game-winning single in the ninth inning – to give Cleveland the close victory over the Oakland A's . . .

After losing the lead, "At least we didn't lay down out there," Ellis said.

"It was a fastball I hit. I hit fastballs all day," he said.

Ellis hit his seventh homer of the season with Charlie Spikes on base in the second inning to give the Tribe a 2-0 edge.

These are scrapbook clippings for sure.

In Detroit weeks later John was still at it. Playing first base, he went five for five at the plate, hitting his ninth homer to open the second inning and then rapping four straight singles, raising his average from .285 to .296.

Then on Sept 28 against the Yankees in Cleveland John went deep to left field and over the fence for the first grand slam of his career. But the game went 9-7 for the Yanks due mostly to a four for five performance, including a double and home run by Roy White.

Ellis had his best season in 1974, when he hit .285 (22nd in the American League), with 23 doubles (25th in the league), and 64 RBI in 128 games.

The Indians announced on Sept. 27 that Aspromonte wouldn't be back as manager. Cleveland was the surprise team of the '74 season, but then slumped late in the season to 4th place. Better than last year's last place, but not good enough for Aspromonte to keep his job.

Enter Frank Robinson, the MVP in both leagues, who was about to get his managerial debut.

Chapter 8
Ellis v. Robinson

Frank Robinson has been called the most underrated baseball superstar of all time. He was fourth on the home run list with 586 behind Hank Aaron (755), Babe Ruth (714) and Willie Mays (660). Think of it this way, he had more career homers than Harmon Killebrew, Reggie Jackson, Mike Schmidt, Mickey Mantle, Ted Williams, and Lou Gehrig, among other sluggers.

On June 26, 1970, Robinson hit two consecutive grand slams for the Orioles against the Washington Senators at RFK Stadium. He had been voted MVP in both leagues, was the American League Triple Crown Winner for Baltimore in 1966 and had a lifetime batting average of .294 over 21 years. But could he manage a team? Cleveland thought so. John Ellis wasn't so sure.

Cleveland grabbed him from the California Angels late in the 1974 season amid speculation that he would become the first Black major league manager. The Indians had signed the first Black American league player, Larry Doby, in 1947 a few months after Brooklyn fielded Jackie Robinson.

On October 3, 1974, Cleveland General Manager Phil Seghi ended the speculation and announced that Robinson would manage the Indians in 1975. The three television networks covered the press conference along with 100 reporters from across the country. Baseball Commissioner Bowie Kuhn and American League President Lee MacPhail were there. President Gerald Ford sent a congratulatory telegram. It was an historic event. Kuhn put the moment in perspective: "Now that it has happened, I'm not going to get up and shout that this is something for baseball to be exceptionally proud of, because it is so long overdue."

Jackie Robinson's widow Rachel was there April 8, 1975 to throw out the first pitch at his first game as manager of the Indians. Jackie Robinson had told a sellout crowd before a World Series game in Cincinnati two years earlier that he hoped to see a Black manager in the imminent future. Rachel said in Cleveland that she was "heartened by this symbol of progress."

She would return again to Municipal Stadium that season to support Frank Robinson in his managerial role. It was just over a decade after the passage of the Civil Rights Act, which ended segregation in public places and banned employment discrimination on the basis of race.

That July, Arthur Ashe became the first African-American to win the British men's singles at Wimbledon, defeating the overwhelming favorite Jimmy Connors.

It was the year the Vietnam War ended with the fall of

Saigon. We were all watching Norman Lear's "All in the Family" and "The Jefferson's," sitcoms filled with characters who "barreled headlong into the most contentious issues of the day," the magazine "Variety" observed. That eminent racist Archie Bunker raised his eyebrow at George Jefferson continually calling white people "honkies."

"I don't think I was hired because I was black," Robinson said at the time. "I hope not. I think I've been hired because of my ability."

The very serious Frank Robinson would be a player-manager, one of the last. Joe Torre was for the Mets in 1977. Pete Rose, for the Reds a decade later, was the last.

Just before opening day 1975, GM Phil Seghi quietly asked Robinson to hit a home run. Robinson rolled his eyes, but in his first at bat, under a national microscope, with two strikes against him and two foul balls, he blasted one into the left field bleachers, electrifying the more than 56,000 fans.

It was Robinson's 575th home run of his career. After the game, when Frank had notched his first managerial win, he told the reporters crowded into his office, "Right now, I feel better than I have after anything I've ever done in this game."

"One hundred thousand fans could not have been louder," he recalled in his memoir. "It was the biggest ovation I ever received, and it almost brought tears to my eyes. After all the years of waiting to become a big league manager — ignored because so many team owners felt that fans would not accept a black manager — I was on the job and people were loudly pleased."

Boog Powell, playing first base, went 3 for 3 that first game.

John Ellis, catching, went two for three and Gaylord Perry walked one and struck out Lou Piniella, Sandy Alomar, Bobby Bonds, and Thurman Munson to beat the Yankees 5 to 3.

Robinson's home run "gave me goose bumps," said Powell. Gaylord Perry was the first out of the Indians' dugout to greet Robinson trotting home. When the game ended with the Indians' 5-3 victory, 56,715 fans responded with a standing ovation. Robinson was the first to greet Perry coming off the field. Both times the two men embraced each other.

The hugging wouldn't last long.

Perry lost a game two weeks later to the Detroit Tigers 6-2, pitching the full game and giving up 12 hits. Ellis was catching and hit a home run in the first inning. He and Perry communed after the game.

"Johnny and I stayed in the dugout and talked. We just talked about the game," said Perry when they finally walked into the clubhouse. "When I jammed 'em, they hit the ball off their fists. When I pitched 'em away, they hit it off the end of their bats. They hit 'em where nobody was. It was frustrating, but it's best not to get upset."

"He broke four bats and two of them became hits," chimed in Ellis.

Robinson walked over to Perry. He shook his hand, said something privately and patted his pitcher on the back. Perry thanked his manager.

Then Robinson said to the beat writers, "Gaylord has been strong and he's pitched well in all four of the games. He could easily have a 4-0 record . . . and I think he'll get even better."

Perry amassed 314 wins and 3,534 strikeouts in his career

and would be elected to the Baseball Hall of Fame in 1991, nine years after Robinson.

According to some observers of the mid-1970s Indians, the team had a clear racial divide. Eight of the team's 40 players that year were Black, including Oscar Gamble, Charlie Spikes and Blue Moon Odom.

Upon his arrival in 1974, Robinson "noted the self-segregation of the team, which even extended to the coaches. This included Larry Doby, the player who'd broken the AL color barrier," wrote Greg Popelka on "Waiting for Next Year."

As the '75 season went on, Robinson began to face opposition from Perry and others for his disciplinarian demeanor. A 21-game winner for the Indians the year before, Perry began to bristle at the manager's conditioning regimen.

"I'm nobody's slave," the North Carolina native said publicly. "The way this place is run is really chicken shit."

Robinson tried to clear things up with his star pitcher in private without success. And it didn't help when Robinson heard that Perry was planning to demand "the same salary, plus a dollar more" than the $173,500 that Robinson was earning.

"To be certain, the two alpha males of the 1975 Cleveland Indians were opposites, culturally and in their personalities. The result was a power struggle that resulted in a mid-season implosion. They hated each other. It was hardly a secret," wrote Popelka, looking back from 2014. "The narrative came easily: the fiery, outspoken black child of the U.S. civil-rights era vs. the white farm boy from the deep South. But was that fair?"

Almost in answer, "The easy scenario is Perry was a white

Southerner from the tobacco fields of North Carolina. Robinson was a bold African-American from California's Bay Area. There was an element of race," wrote sports writer Terry Pluto on Cleveland.com in 2019.

By mid-season the Perry brothers were both traded, Jim to Toronto, Gaylord to the Texas Rangers.

Things got even worse between the 39-year-old manager and his 26-year-old catcher John Ellis. The two had been feuding on-and-off since the start of the season.

Ellis missed the take sign in the 6-0 loss to Milwaukee June 20 and Robinson fined him $100. His next at bat he missed the sign again and Robinson fined him $200 more.

Less than a month later Ellis went 0-3 and Robinson removed him from the game for a pinch hitter. Ellis objected and Robinson felt he was so abusive that he sent him to the dressing room. The slumping Ellis was batting .217.

"He will never become the regular catcher no matter what he does," said his manager. "It's a mutual agreement. He says he can't play for me and I agree." The Indians were looking to trade Ellis and more than a couple of teams were interested.

The Ellis/Robinson baseball tale has endured. John Rosengren wrote in The May/June 2007 edition of The History Channel Magazine:

> "A newspaper story suggested that race was the underlying factor in the dispute. Cleveland fans phoned the Indians switchboard to support Ellis and lobby for Frank's dismissal. Letters to editors of the two Cleveland dailies supported Ellis and criticized Robinson. Seghi stood by Robinson, but it was clear that if lines were to be drawn over race in

Cleveland, the black man would fall on the short side. Frank faced opposition around the country as well. Bigots littered his mailbox with hate mail, and at least two issued death threats that season. One called the Indians' switchboard in June and told the operator, 'If that nigger shows up tonight, we're going to kill him."

John Ellis emphasizes, insists, he has no racial animus and never did. A racist would never invite Roy White, Hank Aaron, Reggie Jackson, Mickey Rivers, Bob Gibson, Jim Rice etc. etc. to headline his cancer foundation fundraising dinners. What Ellis wanted in 1975 was to play baseball. He sought out Russell Schneider of the Cleveland Plain Dealer.

"I want to give you my side of the story of what happened between Robinson and me, but I don't want you to write it until after I'm traded. I want my friends to know I'm not the bad guy Robinson is making me out to be. There were circumstances that brought this thing to a head," Ellis said to Schneider. The sports writer put John's account in his 1976 book, "Frank Robinson The Making of a Manager."

When the Perry brothers were still with the club Robinson advised them and Ellis how to pitch to certain batters. In the game, the Perry's would go against Robinson and he'd complain to Ellis, who told him to talk to the pitchers.

The book detailed an escalating chasm between manager and player -- Robinson accusing Ellis of not relaying his pitch calls to the pitchers - a slider away, for example, that came in as a fastball; Robinson calling Ellis a liar; Robinson fining Ellis $300 for missing two take signs at bat; Ellis asking Robinson if they can work together, but his manager responding "all you want to do is kiss the pitchers' asses."

Schneider also wrote that Indians GM Phil Seghi had talked to eight different clubs about Ellis.

A few weeks later John was back in the lineup, "Because he's willing to play the game the way I want it played – for the good of the team – which is all I ever wanted of him," said Robinson.

In one week of playing, Ellis got six hits, including a home run and a double in 17 at bats, raising his batting average to .234. For the season going into August he had 65 hits – 10 doubles, a triple and seven homers.

For good measure, on Aug. 4 his son, John Jr., was born. Ten days later in a game against the White Sox, John went 2 for 3 with a home run, but reinjured his hamstring and was put on the 15-day disabled list.

John played in 92 games in 1975, hit .230 with seven home runs and 32 RBI, substantially down from his .285 average, 10 homers and 64 RBI in 128 games the year before. He was traded Dec. 9 to Texas (rejoining Gaylord Perry) for Ron Pruitt, a catcher, and Stan Thomas, a pitcher.

Robinson managed the Indians to a 79-80 record in 1975 and an 81-78 record in 1976, their first winning season since 1968. He was fired the next year and reporters asked if he thought race had anything to do with his dismissal.

"If race was a factor I'm not aware of it. I never heard a serious remark about race. I never heard secondhand of anyone making a remark. I have no bitterness about Cleveland. I did the best I could," he said. "I'm looking forward to the day . . . when people will stop writing 'Frank Robinson, baseball's first black manager, and just write, 'Frank Robinson, manager of the Cleveland Indians. It's a fact. It's happened. Save the identification for my epitaph."

He managed for 16 years until he was 70 years old with the Indians, Giants, Orioles, Expos and Nationals, amassing a 1,065-1,176 record, mostly with under-talented teams.

Chapter 9
A Texas Ranger

John Ellis began the 1976 season plastering pitches for a .419 batting average in his first 11 games. Then came the trip to Boston.

If you see it in slow motion . . . On Saturday, May 8 at Fenway Park in the second game of a double header, John is catching and goes 3 for 5 at the plate. Texas wins both games.

The next day, Sunday afternoon before 18,618 fans, John is hitting second as DH. His first at bat he flies out to right field. In the third inning, Cecil Cooper and Jim Rice homer off Gaylord Perry.

John responds in the 4th inning, slamming a homer over the left field wall off Bill Lee. He comes up in the fifth and singles to center. Texas will beat Boston 6-5, but as Toby Harrah singles, John runs for second.

"I was going to slide into second base when I saw the second baseman (Denny Doyle) had missed the ball and then I started to change. I hit the corner of the bag with my left leg and something popped," John said at the time. He broke his left leg and ankle, wanted to walk off the field, but was carried out on a stretcher.

"In the ambulance I said 'give me a cocktail'," John remembers saying 43 years later. "Brad Corbett, the Texas owner sees me in the hospital and says 'we'll operate in Texas.' He puts me on his personal jet. I was leading the league in batting average."

Back in Texas, he says his doctors declared the operation "a complete success." By July he'll have a small fiberglass form-fitted cast and "I'll be able to walk with it . . . They tell me I'll be able to get full mobility when I return to action."

He practiced full mobility with his 7-year-old daughter Erika. "When he broke his leg, he'd race me on crutches," she said with a big smile four decades later.

John's target date in 1976: Sept. 1 as designated hitter and "maybe I can deliver a few clutch hits and help us win the pennant."

His doctors warned he may have to give up catching, but the 27-year-old Ranger rejoined, "I'm sure I'll be able to catch again." Since getting out of the hospital he worked out two or three times a week at the Rangers fitness center.

But September arrived and the doctors advised against playing. All winter Ellis worked out every day at the New London YMCA. When spring training arrived for the 1977 season, "I haven't been able to follow a complete therapy program," the now veteran major leaguer told The Day of New London, "but I'm still optimistic that I will be able to make it all the way back."

The Rangers "have been in touch with me constantly over the winter to check on my progress and have told me they are counting on me as a designated hitter . . . I intend to show them that I can do it."

But he didn't really get the chance. He played in only 49 games, hit .235 with four homers in 119 at bats. The next year wasn't much better: 34 games, 94 at bats, 3 homers and a .245 average.

"When I became the bullpen catcher I read a lot of real estate books. It gets really boring in the bullpen. Some guys listened to music. I read about real estate," John said from the vantage point of a long look back over the years.

Then came 1979 and watch out!

"The point had come where I had to ask myself 'What am I doing here?' I didn't want to hang around if I couldn't hit, but I still had confidence that under the right conditions I would produce," John told Randy Galloway of The Dallas Morning News.

In spring training he went to Manager Pat Corales and told him he'd hit around .280, drive in more than 50 runs and give him some home run power.

"He had to be skeptical. Everybody was because it had been three years since I'd played even on a spot basis. Heck, I had some inner doubts myself. So I worked hard and earned the chance to play when Pat felt I was needed," he said.

John's pale blue eyes look off somewhere. He wasn't in the room sitting for an interview. He saw himself swinging and hitting a fast-pitched ball. He looked over and said in a surprisingly soft voice, "I can see things you can't."

"Ellis Stars for Rangers" rang the headline on a spring training game in 1979. He hit a home run and three singles to lead the Texas Rangers against the Houston Astros 11-7. "Ellis has big night," was the headline when he knocked in six runs on a pair of home runs and a ground-rule double to lead the Rangers 7-1 over the Milwaukee Brewers.

John did better than he had promised his manager. He truly awakened in 1979, with a .285 average, 12 homers, 61 RBI in 316 at bats in 111 games.

Mid-season that year John signed a two-year pact with "a significant increase in pay," his agent Robert W. Marrion of Niantic, announced. Two years earlier John was making $51,000 according to the Baseball Almanac. The raise was to $250,000, according to John, the same as pitcher Doc Medich made that year. Teammate Oscar Gamble pulled down $475,000 that year. (The Rangers said their records don't go back that far). Average MLB salaries jumped from $44,676 in 1975 to $143,746 in 1980 according to Baseball Reference.

In 1979, Texas General Manager Eddie Robinson said, "The Rangers have a very special feeling for John. The young players look upon John as the elder statesman of the team even though there are older players on the roster."

On many levels, major league baseball is a family event whether you're in the stands or in the dugout. It was probably that year when Ellis' 4-year-old son John Jr. started going into the clubhouse where "I'd hang out with Pat Corales or Buddy Bell. On family day I saw the Blue Jays label on the right field fence. I loved blue jays. I ran out there to look at it. 'Bubba' was written on my shirt. The fans in right field started chanting

'Bubba, Bubba'. My father had to go out there and grab me."
Good thing the game wasn't in progress.

His big sister Erika loved Mickey Rivers (15 years, .295 career batting average) who had been traded by the Yankees to Texas.

"I loved the way he twirled his bat," she said, "just like I twirled my baton!"

She can still see herself getting on the team plane with him. "He put a blanket across two seats for me," she remembered decades later.

When Erika was 11 in 1981, she and her father didn't know it, but he was in his last year as a major leaguer. He would play in only 23 games that year, yet as the season opened he told a hometown reporter before a game, "I'm dependable. I've been a bench player. I know the idea is just going up there knowing what to do. Basically my job is as a pinch hitter."

Three hours later in the 8th inning Ellis was called upon to face the Yankees' Tommy John. He hit the first pitch to the base of the right field wall, but into Lou Piniella's glove.

Spring training 1982 was John's last. He was released by Texas Manager Don Zimmer. Nearly four decades later John had a far away look, he scowled, he choked up, but caught himself as he quietly swallowed these words: "Zimmer released me."

It was as if he still couldn't believe it.

Yet, he said matter-of-factly another time, "I was a pro. I could hit, catch at a major league level. But once I realized I wasn't going to be a big star, it was like I was putting in the time. Great players have their own world."

Don Zimmer would become a big champion of the Cancer Foundation. When Zimmer died in 2014 John went to the lectern at the annual dinner.

"When we lost Don Zimmer in June, we lost one of the greats — a great family man, a great baseball man, a great friend of the Foundation. But true legends never die, and Zim will always be remembered," he said.

It can be said that John Ellis, in a 13-year major league career, had two or three great years. His last year with the Yankees in 1972 he hit .294 in 52 games. Twice he hit .285 for the season. From 1969 to 1981 he played in 883 major league games. He caught 297 games, played first base in 304 games and was DH in 169 games. He totaled 699 hits, 116 doubles, 13 triples, 69 home runs, 391 RBI and a .262 lifetime batting average.

"It's not easy going down there and facing some young player who's going to get your job. But these are tests you have to apply to life," he told The Day of New London in March 1982. "And the tests of life are much more difficult than those of playing baseball. You'll face tests all your life."

His career was put in perspective at an early Cancer Foundation dinner by the emcee that night, Reid MacCluggage, the editor and publisher of The Day, John's hometown newspaper.

"Did you know," chimed MacCluggage, "that John hit over .270 six times in his 13-year career? And in 1974, just to pick a year at random, his .285 batting average was higher than Hank Aaron, Pete Rose, Al Kaline, Harmon Killebrew, Willie McCovey, Frank Robinson, Mike Schmidt, Thurman Munson, Johnny Bench, George Brett, Dave Parker, Jim Rice, Billy

Williams, Dave Winfield, Robin Yount, and Graig Nettles!"

And furthermore, said MacCluggage, "Reggie Jackson had one RBI for every five at-bats. John had one for every six. Reggie's lifetime batting average is .262. John's is .262 . . . and John had more assists, fewer errors and a higher fielding average than Reggie."

It was John who introduced a smiling Reggie that night at the dinner.

Chapter 10
Superman Becomes Clark Kent

Pitcher Fritz Peterson and John Ellis were teammates on the Yankees, the Indians and the Texas Rangers. In 11 major league years, Peterson was a 20-game winner with a 2.90 earned run average in 1970 for New York. His career won-loss record was 133-131.

After both Peterson and Ellis were long retired, Peterson took note of John's strength as an athlete, his innate intelligence, his uncanny ability to call a game behind home plate – "better than Thurman Munson." John Ellis was a thinker on the baseball diamond who later in his career studied thick real estate investment books in the bullpen, said the pitcher.

John was reading those heavy books just about anywhere.

"Out in the bullpen, it got boring," he remembered. "Most guys listened to music. I brought my real estate books. I read out there."

It began in a not-so-great neighborhood in New London.

"Growing up we lived in a two-family place. I saw my father paying rent. Every month, money to the owner . . ." It made obvious sense to the teenager – every month cash came in. At a young age the kid not only could hit, he could add and subtract.

At 17 in 1966 John bought a brand new GTO with his Yankees signing bonus. On Oct. 16, 1970, after swatting 56 hits, including seven homers, in 78 games, John made his first real estate investment. He put $5,000 down on a duplex on Warren Street in New London.

His mortgage payment was $164 a month. He collected twice that from his tenants.

"So I bought two. Then I bought maybe five or six more in the neighborhood, collected rent for 10-15 years. Then sold them. I made a profit, probably a couple hundred thousand dollars," said John. Maybe closer to $300,000.

As a 29-year-old major leaguer, "I was in spring training closing properties on the phone." Back then, "There was more money in real estate" than in baseball, he said.

He remembers how during his 10th year in the majors, one of his worst -- playing in only 34 games with 94 at bats, only 23 hits and three homers – he scored: "Probably my first large acquisition, an apartment building worth $300,000. A lot of money," he said.

The local newspaper was covering not only his baseball career, but now his real estate activity too:

"John Ellis firm buys apartments Jan 20 1978

The firm headed by Texas Ranger ballplayer John Ellis has purchased one apartment building in Montville. John Ellis and

Associates, established in New London last year, made the final payments this month and took ownership of the 24-unit Lakeside Manor apartments on Fellows Road . . . His father Louis Ellis who works with his son occasionally said expanding by 12 or 24 units has been talked about."

John Ellis remembers it this way 42 years later. Ellis and Associates included his friend Gary Leitkowski. His blue eyes twinkling, John paused, pondered, then said, "The main supporting beam was rotting." He smiled. "Gary and I jacked up the building and replaced the beam." He paused again, then with a big grin, said "We probably couldn't do that today."

No kidding. There'd be permits, and inspections and hiring contractors with proper equipment, and so on.

John doesn't remember if the replacement beam was wood or steel.

Retired Hartford Courant sports columnist Bob Sudyk, (who covered John in Cleveland when Sudyk wrote for the Cleveland Press) put it this way in 1988: Ellis's "indomitable spirit and creative financial mind" have "dwarfed his accomplishments in baseball. He directs a multimillion dollar residential-commercial real estate partnership. Employs 100. Manages-owns 3,000 office and housing rental units . . . He has an apartment in Manhattan, another in Florida, a farm in Maine and a home on Long Island Sound.

"His successful real estate career was simultaneously launched with his baseball career. 'I made more money in each off-season than I earned in uniform,' said Ellis, whose initial $8,000 salary grew to $150,000," Sudyk wrote.

Pause a moment. Some of this is lost in the mists of time

and John Ellis's changing memory. The New York Yankees and Texas Rangers say the decades-old documentation is gone. So John either signed for an initial $8,000 or $10,000. His bonus was either $20,000 or $25,000 or $50,000. His highest baseball salary was either $150,000 or $185,000 or $250,000.

Sudyk ended up painting it this way:

"Some remember the always muddied, brawling, nose-in-the-dirt dead-end kid who crashed into second base like a bullet train and protected home plate as if he were brick and mortar. They should see Mr. Ellis now in his dark silk suit, patent leather shoes and power necktie. It is Superman entering the phone booth to become Clark Kent."

Two months after Ellis bought Lakeside Apartments in 1978, The Day of New London reported:

"Pattagansett Apartments sold

Twelve garden apartments in Niantic were sold to Pattagansett Associates of New London, part of John Ellis Associates, for $220,000. Ellis is a Texas Ranger."

The deals kept coming and got a little more complicated. In 1982 John purchased a 34-unit complex, again in Montville, Conn. for $630,000. Ownership changed hands twice in one week that January. Initially sold by John F. Carr to John C. Ellis and then for the same amount from Ellis to Montview Associates. The newspaper reported Ellis declined to name the principals in the partnership.

"It is just a group of people who feel the property is the type they wanted," he said.

And then it got bigger. Across the Thames River in Ledyard,

John, four years out of baseball in 1985, bought the 212-unit Highland Park apartments for nearly $1.8 million. A year later, "We sold 40 of the units to another buyer and returned $1.4 million to our investors and we still owned 170 of the units – all those rents coming in!

"A main goal is to return clients' funds in a five-year period and to still own the property," he told The Day back then.

About this time Aetna loaned Ellis about $18 million in non-recourse funding, a type of commercial lending that entitles the lender to repayment only from the profits of the project the loan is funding and not from any other assets of the borrower. It was a coup of sorts for Ellis.

John Ellis & Associates, "is moving aggressively into Palm Beach County, FL and southern Maine on the well-researched assumption that they are major growth areas," The Day reported Sept. 21, 1986.

Ellis, then 35, had formed a partnership in 1983 with Peter I. Leibowitz of New London, who was 40. Their partnership grew from less than a half dozen employees to more than 80, including 26 in Florida.

"It's been determined by the Brookings Institute that Maine has the lowest real estate prices in all the United States," said Ellis, "companies are moving into the Portland area and south because of its quality of life and accessibility to major markets."

The firm is buying two large brick apartment complexes in Bath, buildings Ellis spotted on his way to his 200-acre farm in Camden, Maine, the newspaper reported.

In Florida, in July 1986 they bought the 542-unit Tanglewood Apartments for $21.8 million and the 22-unit time-share condo complex, Juno Shores resort, for $2.3 million. Both are in Palm Beach Gardens.

Leibowitz was away for the Tanglewood deal, Ellis said with that twinkle in his eyes. If he wasn't so big, you'd think he was a leprechaun. Vincent Pappalardo owned Tanglewood. He was one of the biggest men in Palm Beach real estate from the mid-1950s to when Ellis arrived. Pappalardo built more than 4,000 custom homes and commercial buildings, including the Holiday Inn, the Radisson Hotel, the Admiralty Hotel, the Northern Palm Beach County Chamber of Commerce edifice, St. Ignatius Cathedral, and Tanglewood.

"Vince wanted $5 million down. We agreed. But I started thinking about it. Peter was away," Ellis explained. "soooo, I go see Pappalardo. I told I'm not closing with $5 million down."

John allows a pregnant pause. "He knocked off $2 million. Peter came back, he was like, shocked!" John says with a big grin.

The vagaries of the economy, the ups and downs in the real estate market, even as he closed on the Tanglewood deal, John was thinking he'd had enough of Florida.

As the economy was tanking, the cancer that took his brother and his sister came after John.

Chapter 11
"I Understand End of Life Issues"

John Ellis's sister Dolores, who had two daughters, died of breast cancer. The year John retired from baseball, in 1982, his big brother Rick, a teacher in New London, died of Hodgkins disease.

"My mother and father were never the same" after Dolores and Rick died, said John.

Four years later, John got it too.

"At 38, it was my turn. 1986. I was living in Florida buying and selling apartment complexes. I was diagnosed with a large mass in my chest."

He met the attractive former social worker turned flight attendant, Jane Gregory, she called Memorial Sloan Kettering in New York.

Hodgkins, third stage in his chest and spleen. They "shot me up with radiation, burned your inside out," John remembered.

"There was a whole team of doctors in John's hospital room. I was waiting outside the room. Out of all of those doctors, Dr. Yahalom took it upon himself to come over to me and said, 'We believe John's diagnosis is Hodgkins Disease and if that is confirmed we will cure him.' I knew right then that John would be fine. The diagnosis was confirmed and Achy treated John with radiation and here we are 34 years later!" said Jane. John and Jane were married June 11, 1988.

In separate interviews, John and Jane are like a mutual admiration society. "John is one of the smartest guys I ever met," said Jane. "He's gregarious, I'm more serious."

John: "I'm dying. I think I'm dying. I'm fighting cancer. I don't expect to live . . . My Jane fought with me. She's an angel on earth," he said. In fact he says that a lot.

"A couple years later there was a tumor in my back. They cut it out and inserted radiation rods in my back and burned up the area. Then I went out and had pizza," said John.

Not generally a quiet man, "I understand end-of-life issues," Ellis said quietly.

Then he was on a roll:

"You know, this whole effort has helped me live longer. I don't understand why people don't care about each other. What right do you have to live unless you help other people? Life is about courage and trust, supporting one another. This is not about a lasting legacy for me, it's about Connecticut cancer patients," he said about founding their cancer foundation.

"I'm helping to the very end. I never expected it to be this big. Jane has inspired me every day. We hope this will be the greatest charity in Connecticut, maybe not in my lifetime, but . . ." said the former major league baseball player.

On May 1, 1987, John and Jane Ellis incorporated the Con-

necticut Sports Foundation, later renamed the Connecticut
Cancer Foundation. The first dinner was Feb. 7, 1988. Enter
Mickey Mantle, Whitey Ford and Billy Martin.

John Ellis American Legion Baseball Champ 1966

THE ELLIS FAMILY — Mr. and Mrs. Louis R. Ellis of 138 Hawthorne Drive will have their son, John, right, home for the winter. Ellis, who wound up a sizzling two weeks with Syracuse in the International League Sunday with a .356 batting average, is scheduled for an operation on the little finger of his right hand.

Courtesy The Day, New London

Off Season

Brothers John (left) and Dave Ellis pose with the family's favorite dog at the Christmas tree lot on Colman St. in New London. It's off-season for both John, a Cleveland Indians baseball player, and Dave, who has just finished his senior year as defensive end for the University of Connecticut football team. (Day Photo by Hubert Warren)

John's brother Dave also survived cancer, was a 1st Lieutenant in the US Marine Corps, a career high school guidance counselor. Courtesy of The Day, New London

HIS BOYS — Harry Hesse, New York Yankees Eastern Scout, signed Tommy Shopay of Bristol (left) and John Ellis of New London (right). The three got together this week when the Yankees had Press Day at the Waverly Inn, Cheshire. Shopay and Ellis are on the Yankee roster and will report for spring training this month.

Ralph Houk and Ellis   Ellis and Thurman Munson

John Ellis Promoted To Syracuse IL Club

NEW LONDON — The New York Yankees have promoted former New London High athlete John Ellis from their Class A Fort Lauderdale entry in the Florida State League to the Syracuse Chiefs of the Class AAA International League.

Ellis' family confirmed the announcement today, reporting their son notified them of the move in a telephone conversation Tuesday night.

The young catcher, now in his second year of professional baseball, has shaken off a series of injuries and misfortunes to fashion an impressive finish in 1968.

A strong August surge saw his batting average climb to .252. His hits include six homers, three triples and 11 doubles.

JOHN ELLIS

John with
Syracuse Chiefs
Manager
Frank Verdi

Torrid Ellis Talks With Manager

Johnny Ellis, returning for the first time since injuring a finger in the first game of a doubleheader Tuesday, continued his torrid hitting for the Syracuse Chiefs Thursday night with four singles and a double as the Chiefs dumped Buffalo, 13-3, in an International League contest. The night gave Ellis, from New London and who was summoned from Fort Lauderdale Aug. 28, 16 hits in 37 appearances for a lofty .432 bat mark. After a six-for-eight night in his first two games for the Chiefs, Ellis has collected a home run which beat Buffalo 2-0, and driven in seven runs. Here he is shown chatting with manager Frank Verdi before a recent game.

76

John Ellis Hitting .432 for Syracuse

SYRACUSE, N. Y. — John Ellis hits singles when he breaks his bat.

When he breaks a finger, he goes on a real batting tear.

Ellis, the former New London High star athlete who was promoted to the Syracuse club of the International League, broke the finger Tuesday night.

But Ellis, who has been through a lot this season that includes being hit by a car and a pitched ball, refused to call it quits.

So instead of coming home, Ellis just picked up a bat Thursday night and pounded out five hits in five times at bat. He had four singles and a double, scored two runs and knocked in one himself.

On his double, Ellis went all around the bases. The throw to second hit him and so he scrambled to third, continuing home when the outfield throw went into the dugout.

Since being promoted to Syracuse, Ellis has hammered out 16 hits in 37 times at bat

for a .432 average. He has one home run and seven runs batted in. His homer won a recent game against Buffalo, 2-0.

Syracuse has a mathematical chance of making the international League playoffs. The Chiefs now trail Jacksonville by three games and have three games left at home against Buffalo. Jacksonville has three doubleheaders left, all on the road against Columbus.

Not only is Ellis hitting the ball well, but he is catching in acceptable fashion, too. Arnie Burdick, sports editor of the Syracuse Herald, said today "we like him (Ellis) very much."

OLD AND NEW — New London's John Ellis and New York Yankee Coach Elston Howard are pictured prior to Wednesday night's New York-Kansas City game at Yankee Stadium. Ellis is making a strong bid to become the regular Yankee catcher, a post Howard held down quite capably for years. (Staff Photo)

Photo courtesy of
The Norwich Bulletin

Dana Tinti, Ansonia Evening Sentinel

Courtesy of Gordon Visselli,
American Legion Post 50,
Ansonia, CT

Photos

John Ellis New York Yankee 1969

Yankee Manager Ralph Houk and John Ellis

John and Thurman made the Topps Baseball Cards Rookie All-star Team in 1970, along with Bernie Carbo, Larry Bowa, Roy Foster, Dave Cash, Billy Conigliaro, Alan Gallagher, Les Cain, and Carl Morton. Cards courtesy of Topps.

The young Ellis and Munson showed kids the finer points of the game.

Photos

Yankee Roy White slides home ahead of Cleveland's John Ellis's tag Sept. 21, 1974. Courtesy of the Associated Press

JUST LIKE DADDY — Erica Ellis, four-year-old daughter of Cleveland Indians' catcher John Ellis who hails from New London, displays some of the rugged diamond play her father is known for as she runs over seven-year-old Deron Williams, son of outfielder Walt Williams, during a Father-Son and Daughter game prior to the Sunday doubleheader with the Texas Rangers.

Like father, like daughter, four-year-old Erika Ellis slides home.

81

Yanks Trade John Ellis to Indians

New London Ace In Six-Player Swap

John Ellis—Soon To Be Swinging for Tribe

1973 A Cleveland Indian

Robinson
and Ellis
clashed in
Cleveland

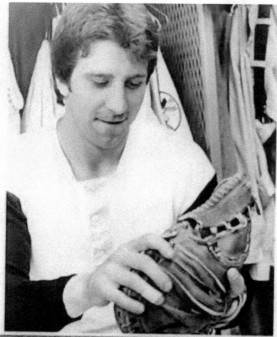

Trying it on
for Cleveland

Courtesy The Day
New London

Former Teammates

Sparky Lyle (left) and John Ellis were roomates when both were members of the New York Yankees baseball team last year. Since then Ellis has been traded to the Cleveland Indians. They met at the Holiday Inn Saturday afternoon. Lyle was in town as guest speaker at the Electric Boat Athletic Club's annual banquet. Ellis, incidently, signed his 1973 Cleveland contract and said he is "extremely happy" with the pact. (Day Photo).

Ellis on Target as Ranger

By RANDY GALLOWAY

ARLINGTON—John Ellis had something important to prove in 1979. After nine years in the majors, he had to show he still could hit a baseball consistently.

"In spring training," said Ellis, "I went to Pat (Manager Corrales) and gave him a set of statistics for the upcoming season. I told him that given the opportunity, I would deliver those numbers for him.

"He had to be skeptical. Everybody was because it had been three years since I'd played even on a split basis. I had some inner doubts myself, doubts that you never express publicly but you know they're there. So I worked hard and earned the chance to play when Pat felt I was needed."

What Ellis told Corrales in the spring was that he'd hit in the vicinity of .280, drive in over 50 runs and give him some home-run power. All these Ellis predictions were based on at least 300 official at-bats.

The final stats show Ellis at the plate 316 times, with a .285 average, 12 homers and 61 RBIs.

[illegible]

The Dallas Morning News

Topps

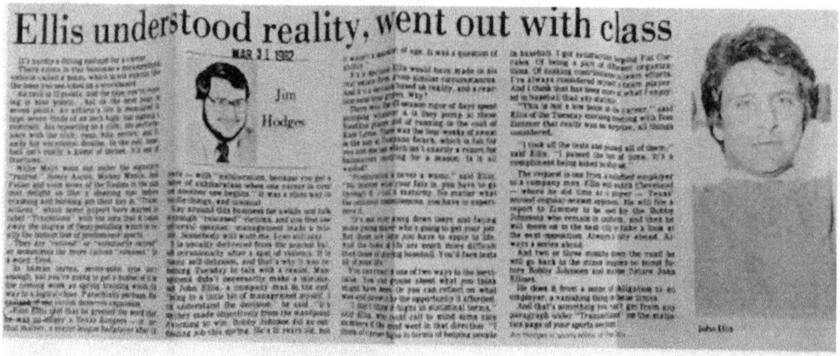

Ellis understood reality, went out with class

MAR 31 1982

Jim Hodges

John Ellis

The Day, New London

And then he went fishing

with Don Zimmer and Mel Stottlemyre

Firm finds success in real estate buys

By Bob Andrews
Day Staff Writer

A New London-based real estate investment company is moving aggressively into Palm Beach County, Fla. and southern Maine properties in the well researched assumption that they are major growth areas that will give southeastern Connecticut investors a strong return.

John Ellis & Associates, founded in New London native and former major league baseball player John Ellis has begun putting millions into Florida and Maine real estate. The company bought the 342-unit Tanglewood Apartments complex in Palm Beach Gardens, Fla. for $21.5 million July 11 and the 22-unit, time-share condominium complex, June Shores Resort in the same city, for $2.3 million July 1. It also has plans to invest $12 million to $20 million in real estate from Boston to southern Maine.

Ellis & Associates, a partnership between Ellis, 38, and Peter I. Leibowitz, 43, of New London, structures limited real estate partnerships that buy and manage apartment complexes, often with the intent of converting them to condominiums over a five-year period.

Approximately 90 percent of its investors are southeastern Connecticut residents, who invest a minimum of $25,000 in a given real estate purchase. The company also operates a commercial and residential real estate business and property management firm from offices at 238 William St. and 29 Bridal St.

The shift represents a change from an emphasis on real estate purchases in southeastern Connecticut, with which the firm has done well. Among the firm's local investments are the Farmington Arms in New London, 74 units converted to condominiums in 1985; Pheasant Hill apartments in Gales Ferry, 44 units converted in 1985 and Christie Hill, 80 units in Gales Ferry converted this year.

"Our future plans are to take people from Connecticut and to be able to offer them investment opportunities in Florida either through real estate acquisition (in limited partnerships) or buying or renting a home," said Ellis, who now resides in East Lyme. "And we want to offer them a full service real estate company within an area of Florida we think is the best growing, Palm Beach County.

"We determined three years ago the prices for apartment (buildings) in Connecticut were becoming too high," said Ellis. The high prices, combined with tax reform legislation and the government's drive to balance its budget, prompted Ellis and his associates to rethink their company's future strategy. They speculate government efforts to balance the

Investors/011

> 'Here's an athlete who spent more than a decade in professional baseball and he has turned this into a multimillion dollar business.'
>
> Peter I. Leibowitz

> 'When you are an athlete, doors are closed to you unless you can prove to people you really know your business. It's only through your track record and experience that you can accomplish that.'
>
> John Ellis

Then John Ellis got cancer like his brother and sister before him. And was saved by this man: Joachim Yahalom, radiation oncologist at Memorial Sloan Kettering Cancer Center in Manhattan.

87

1988 - First Celebrity Dinner

"I hope this goes on forever" - Mickey Mantle

Mickey Mantle and Jane Ellis at the first Foundation dinner 1988.

2004 dinner
Whitey Ford, Mel Stottlemyre, Don Zimmer, Johnny Damon, Jason Giambi, Jeremy Giambi, Hank Bauer, Moose Skowron

1990 dinner
Erika Ellis, John Ellis, John Ellis Jr., Don Mattingly, Mike Pagliarulo, Bucky Dent, Jane Ellis

Broadcaster Mike Francesa with Bernie Williams before the 2015 dinner.

Connecticut artist Patrick Ganino and Gary Sanchez with Ganino's portrait of the Yankee catcher at the 2020 dinner.

Central Connecticut State University police, l-r: Sergeants Jerry Erwin, Thomas Gray, Lieutenant Chris Cervoni, Sergeant Densil Samuda, Lieutenant Orlando Oliveira, Chief Gregory Sneed.

Vernon police, left to right: Officers Marindino, Seinbersky, Flannigan, Vogt, Roberge, St. Pierre, Toce and Sgt. Tedford of the evening shift. All three shifts participated as well as administrative staff. "Normally our uniform standards don't allow for full beards due to the officers having to possibly wearing protective masks. No Shave November is a union fundraiser for which I waived the clean shave requirements," Chief James L. Kenny

CARL YASTRZEMSKI

From his debut in 1961 to his retirement in 1983 to his induction in the Baseball Hall of Fame on July 23, 1989, Carl Yastrzemski was and still is one of the most beloved Red Sox players of all time.

During his legendary career, Yaz compiled numbers that gave him a top-10 ranking in eight of baseball's offensive categories and made him the first American League player to reach the 3,000-hit and 400-home run milestone. One of the game's great clutch hitters, the Long Island native batted .417 with six home runs and 25 runs batted in during 22 pennant-deciding and post-season games.

Perhaps his crowning achievement, though, is a 1967 performance that stands as one of the greatest individual season-long efforts of all time. During that incredible year, Yaz batted .326 with 44 home runs and 121 RBI to win the Triple Crown. He also led the American League in slugging percentage at .622, in total bases at 360, in runs at 112 and in hits with 189. There was little wonder when he was named the AL's player of the year and Most Valuable Player.

The 1998 program featuring Carl Yastrzemski.

Jane with a check for a family hit by cancer.

Big Papi David Ortiz with two fans at the 2017 dinner.

Above: John, Jane and Derek Jeter
at the 2018 dinner.

Right: Jeter with Connecticut artist Marc
Potocsky with his portrait of the retired
shortstop. Host Michael Kay in a live
auction sold it for $15,000.

Foundation headquarters and Hall of Fame in Old Saybrook, CT

The late Vince Genovese's daughter Karol, through the Vincent Genovese Memorial Foundation, donated $250,000 to build the museum and hall of fame in the new foundation office building in Old Saybrook.

Whitey Ford at the 2004 dinner with the author and Elizabeth White Notarangelo, now the publisher and executive vice president of the Record-Journal in Meriden, CT. Her father Eliot White, Record-Journal president, was a foundation vice president and board member.

Chapter 12
Mickey, Whitey and Billy

The first charity dinner featured three baseball immortals. And 39-year-old John Ellis was worried. No matter that the steady hand of Joe Stellato, a guy who started his own bank and made it a success, was the first president of the foundation.

No matter that Joe himself volunteered to drive a limo into Manhattan to fetch Mickey Mantle and Billy Martin. (Whitey Ford 's son was driving him to Groton).

Stellato, looking back three decades later, surrounded by signed baseball photos all over the walls of his Niantic, Conn. condo, including both Thurman Munson and John Ellis at bat, cracked a big grin.

"That Sunday morning John is a wreck. He says, 'I know these guys, they're gonna drink and drink and not show up!'"

Stellato leaves early with the limo and gets to the Pierre Hotel in Manhattan where Martin was staying. It's 8:30 in the morning and Martin and Mantle are in the bar signing baseballs for that night's dinner, as they were asked to do -- and drinking.

"They were putting down Bloody Marys one after the other. I said to myself 'how are these guys going to stand up'?" said Stellato.

Ellis was getting more and more nervous. He drives down to New York and finds Stellato.

"I know these guys! They're not going to come!" John says again. He parks out on the street and asks Stellato to come out of the Pierre and give him the "safe sign" every hour until 2 p.m. when they'd head for Connecticut. Stellato gives John the sign each hour and at 2 p.m. Billy and Mickey got in the limo and kept signing baseballs on the drive east.

They arrived for a pre-dinner $750 per-person private reception. A success that would be repeated at every dinner afterwards -- except that someone stole the three boxes of signed baseballs.

"I don't know how they got more, but at the head table during dinner Mickey, Billy and Whitey were signing baseballs as they ate. That's how gracious they were, " said Stellato, "They did such a great job with stories at the dinner."

Yes they did, and helped raise $100,000 for the fledgling foundation.

"I hope this goes on forever," Mantle said of the foundation.

The Mick, 20 years out of the game where he hit 536 home runs in 18 years, was a baseball analyst for Channel 11 TV in New York. Ford was also retired 20 years. He had a 236 -106 lifetime record and in 1961 won both the Cy Young Award (with 25 wins) and the World Series Most Valuable Player Award. He was prepped for a tale or two this night to the 400 people packing the dining room at the Groton Motor Inn.

But first came a press conference with the Yankees new manager, Billy Martin, just hired for the fifth time to lead the club. He was 59 and he said, "we're going to be getting back to the way the Yankees were when we first joined the team – the dress code, the way you act when you are a Yankee. I have strong rules. I'm a very strict person when it comes to rules…

"I'm a gambler as a manager, too – I'm not afraid to stick my neck out on the block to create some runs. You can't always wait for the big inning," he declared.

As dinner began, former New London Mayor Harvey Mallove gave a welcome and talked of how sports are "part of the fabric of America."

"For a couple of hours winter stood still," wrote The Day's Brian Hallenbeck in a Page One story the next day. "Time was even turned back. Years, no, decades, fell away. It was 1950 and Ford was striking out the Red Sox' Walt Dropo (a local boy who was seated at a table in the middle of the room) on the last day of Dropo's Rookie of the Year season . . .

"It was spring training 1968, and Mantle, about to begin his 18th and final season, was asking a rookie to critique his swing. That rookie, who informed the Mick he was 'lunging at the ball,' was John Ellis."

It was Whitey who grabbed the microphone after dinner, announcing that he was taking them all back to 1959, Yankees v. White Sox in New York.

"Nellie Fox is first up. First pitch he hits a double. Then Luis Aparicio. My second pitch he bunts safely. Then Minnie Minoso. I throw a hell of a curve and hit him in the knee cap.

99

Three pitches and the bases are loaded."

The legendary Chairman of the Board pauses and waits for the laughter to die down.

"Ted Kluszewski comes up and hits a high fastball off the right-center field wall. Three runs score. Casey (Stengel) comes out to the mound. And Yogi doesn't want to miss anything, comes out too.

"Casey says to Yogi, 'does Whitey have anything?

"Yogi says, 'How the hell do I know, I haven't caught a pitch yet!"

It is safe to report that Whitey brought down the house that night.

But Mickey wouldn't be out done.

He starts out with that hint of a drawl and says that Billy had wanted to go hunting. "Well I knew this rancher, big ranch down in Texas. Billy and I drive down there in the pick-up truck, six hours. I tell Billy to wait in the truck, I knock on my friend's door.

"He says sure we can hunt, but could I do him a favor and shoot that old ailing mule out back. I agreed.

"I go get Billy and say, "C'mon, that old SOB won't let us hunt. I take Billy around in back and shoot the mule.

"Then I hear three shots – blam-blam-blam -- and turn to Billy.

"He says, 'I just shot three of the bastard's cows!"

Yep, the place exploded in laughter. The Foundation had found its dinner strategy.

The players made the dinners work. In the early years, they each received $10,000 from the foundation (Whitey Ford returned half of his fee). Even the great major leaguers prior to the 1970s didn't make much money. In answer to a question, the Mick put it in perspective:

"The most I ever made in my life was $100,000 and Don Mattingly makes $2 million," he said at the inaugural 1988 dinner.

Mattingly had just finished his sixth season. He batted .327 with 30 homers. He bested the Mick with a .307 lifetime batting average to Mick's .298, but played four fewer years. Donnie Baseball won the American League MVP in 1985; Mantle was most valuable player three times. Perhaps nodding his cap to the Mick, in 2011 Mattingly launched his first fundraising event for his charity serving underprivileged youth at Mickey Mantle's Restaurant on Central Park South.

Chapter 13
The Aflac Duck

Whitey Ford became a foundation board member and John asked who they could invite to the next dinner.

"I mentioned Joe and Yogi and we got in touch with them and we were lucky, they said 'yes' right away," said Whitey. Even though it was no secret that Joe DiMaggio could be irascible, it was the same drill as the year before, foundation board member and bank president Joe Stellato would drive to Manhattan in a limo and pick up Hall of Famers Berra and DiMaggio.

They are both baseball immortals, but it was DiMaggio who Simon and Garfunkel sang about:

"Where have you gone Joe DiMaggio, our nation turns its lonely eyes to you . . .
What's that you say, Mrs. Robinson, Joltin' Joe has left and gone away . . . "

DiMaggio was there when Stellato knocked on his hotel

room door at 10:30 a.m. to tell him the limo was his until they had to leave at 2 p.m. The Yankee Clipper was in his bathrobe and slippers and told Stellato, in no uncertain terms, to scram.

Stellato met Yogi and his wife Carmen Berra for lunch.

"Of all the celebrities he was the most unpretentious guy you ever want to meet," the bank president said of Berra.

Later in the limo DiMaggio asked about John Ellis, "who the hell is this guy anyway?"

"Yogi and I explained he played for the Yankees," said Stellato. "I handed DiMaggio my card – "President and CEO" of a bank. There was a transformation. He was so nice. Me, DiMaggio and Yogi talking about baseball" on the ride to the foundation dinner.

So, what's a baseball book without strange stats? Ellis and DiMaggio had this in common: They were very young Yankees who hit more home runs in a season than other young Yankees.

In 1936 when he was a 21-year-old rookie, Joe hit 29 homers in 637 at bats. In 1970 when he was a 21-year-old rookie, Ellis hit 7 homers in 226 at bats.

Two decades before Ellis performed the rookie feat, Mickey Mantle did it in 1951 – 13 homers. And in 1952 – 23 homers, and 1953 – 21 homers; more than any other Yankee under 22-years-old. It's the young sluggers stat. Other young Yankee sluggers who hit the most homers on the team before age 22 include Lou Gehrig, Yogi Berra, Bobby Murcer, Willie Randolph, Tony Kubek, Frank Crosetti, and Joe Pepitone.

In his 18-year career, Mantle hit 536 home runs, 18th on the all-time list. DiMaggio, who lost three years to World War 11, had 361 homers in 13 years.

Maybe he shouldn't have been Joltin' Joe. Maybe he should have been bashful Joe.

At the dinner DiMaggio "wouldn't walk through the room. He went through the kitchen in back to the head table. He said 'you have to protect me'," said Stellato.

He also didn't want to sign baseballs. "My hand hurts," he said and signed only three. "John talked to him and he signed a few more."

But, "he was a great speaker," according to his limo driver.

And he was. Personable, relaxed, knowledgeable, even funny, Joe D was 75 but looked 20 years younger seated at the head table with Whitey, who joined the Yankees in 1950, the year before Joe retired, and Yogi who came up in 1946 and played six years with Joe.

"I'd like to tell you about Yogi," is the way DiMaggio began that night, after saying with a certain sincerity, "I'm very happy to be here with my two ex-teammates."

"Yogi did a great job behind the plate but sometimes Casey (Stengel) would put him in right field. Yogi would roam a little too far out there. A fly ball was coming to me in center. I was under the ball about to catch it when all of a sudden I get hit – Pow!"

Joltin' Joe brought the house down with that one. No one even wondered whether he hung on to the ball or not. Master of Ceremonies Harvey Mallove had just introduced him as a player of "grace and dignity" and how he wasn't really "joltin'," he was "smooth and effortless" on the ballfield.

DiMaggio was seated between Whitey and John Ellis. Whitey began speaking with this: "Since I was 8-years-old he was my hero. Joe DiMaggio was the greatest ballplayer of all time."

The great DiMaggio was still eating, but he stopped long enough for a quick glance and a smile at Whitey.

Of course he was asked about his 56-game hitting streak and he remembered there were a "a couple of times it looked like the end of it." In one game he was hitless in his first two at bats. "The third time up I got a base hit and I was very fortunate to get that base hit."

Years later it looked like Pete Rose was closing in on him with some 45 consecutive games. But Pete struck out swinging the next game and complained "he should have given me something to hit!," said DiMaggio.

He paused and said to the 400 dinner guests that night, "Well, that's how it goes. You do it and then you don't do it." His record has stood for 79 years.

Yogi was a distinctive speaker. Bill Dickey "learned me all his experience," Yogi famously said of the man who preceded him behind the plate.

He told the rapt audience at the Groton Motor Inn that, "I learned a lot playing in New London, it was like Triple A ball." He was 19-years-old in the U.S. Navy and hit .443 for the now defunct Morgan League, drawing the attention of Yankee scouts.

A year earlier he was a machine gunner on a landing craft support boat in the D-Day invasion of Normandy. Berra earned a Purple Heart, a Distinguished Unit Citation, two battle stars and a European Theatre of Operations ribbon during the war.

Dickey too, was in the Navy, and came back as the Yankees' player/manager in 1946 and showed Yogi how to be a major league catcher. Both of them, of course, are in the Baseball Hall of Fame.

Yogi Berra came back many times to the foundation dinners. One year, board member and Mohegan tribal leader Maynard Strickland wanted Yogi to sign, not a baseball, but something else.

Yogi had been featured in the Aflac insurance company's Aflac duck commercials on television: "They give you cash, which is just as good as money."

Strickland had "this big old Aflac duck in my basement. It was as big as I was. I asked John what if I brought it in and had Yogi sign it."

Yogi had no objection. "Have him bring it in, I'll sign it," said Yogi.

"He signed it right on the beak," said Strickland.

Chapter 14
Parade of Champions

In 1992 pitchers Gaylord Perry and Sparky Lyle; shortstop-turned manager Gene "Stick" Michael; John McNamara, who managed six teams in 20 years including Boston and Cleveland; and sportscaster Howard Cosell were the featured guests at the annual dinner. The biggest ovation was for the 74-year-old Cosell who had recently beat cancer.

He loudly thanked, "whatever gods that may be," but admitted, "I'll not pretend this past year has been easy for me."

He retired that year and said, "I've got nothing left to prove."

Either did Gaylord Perry, who pitched for 22 years, won 314 games, lost 265 for eight different teams and was voted into the Baseball Hall of Fame in 1991. Mid-way through his career in 1974 Perry wrote a book with sportswriter Bob Sudyk, appropriately titled, "Me & the Spitter." He took note that it was necessary for he and his catcher, John Ellis, to understand each other.

They did. Batters watched baseballs drop a foot and half. Opposing managers would rant and rave at umpires. And Perry just kept stacking up wins.

At the foundation dinner John introduced Gaylord. "I'm proud to say he made the Hall of Fame. I'm proud to say I caught a few of his games and I'm proud to say he threw a spit-ball."

Perry was back at the dinner in 1994, the first at the Mashantucket Pequot Casino. Berra, Ford and Sparky Lyle were back, along with Bob Gibson, Doc Ellis, Mickey Rivers, Gene Michael, Buck Showalter, and Joe Pepitone. They raised $75,000 for the foundation.

Rivers, young Erika Ellis's buddy who brought the baton-like twirl of the bat from the on deck circle to the batter's box, said this night, a decade after he retired, "I want to be remembered as someone who always came through when it counted." Usually he did. He stole 70 bases, more than anyone else in 1975. In seven of his 15 years in the game he hit over .300, including .326 for the Yankees in 1977 and .391 in the ALCS.

Perry and Michael were back the next year with Yankees Manager Buck Showalter, Red Sox great Jim Rice, and Reggie "Mr. October" Jackson. It was after the bitter strike that ended the 1994 season in August and it still wasn't clear if the '95 season would open on time, though Showalter said he was hopeful. Rice offered that his job as hitting instructor "is probably more enjoyable than when I played."

It was nearly 20 years earlier when Jackson hit three homers on three pitches clinching Game 6 of the 1977 World Series against the L.A. Dodgers. That's when he became Mr. October.

He is 14th on the all-time list with 563 home runs. But this January night Mr. October declined to comment to newspaper reporters.

The dinners then were more like a baseball carnival -- boys and girls running around with baseballs in their hands looking for major league signatures. You could run into a Bob Gibson or a Buck Showalter just by wandering around. Often the kids didn't wander, they dashed, exclaiming, "I got Boomer Scott!"

"Yeah – well I got Jim Rice!"

And it wasn't just kids. A grizzled almost gnarly Don Larsen was walking and limping down the hall near the silent auction back then, carrying a scotch on the rocks. A guy walked up to him holding out a baseball.

"Hey Don! Can I get your autograph?"

The 1956 World Series hero gazed for a moment, then barked, "Hold this drink!"

The guy did.

"Gimme that ball! And a pen!"

He signed it, retrieved his scotch and meandered away.

Many players were seated at tables facing long lines of fans looking for autographs. One fellow waited for Willie Randolph at the 2005 event. He had an action photo of Willie in his hand. At his turn the dinner guest said, "Hi Willie, you were my daughter Steph's favorite player. Could you sign this for her?

He smiled, asked for the correct spelling, and wrote "To Steph. All my best. Willie Randolph."

Chapter 15
Dining with the Stars

The 1996 foundation dinner emcee Reid MacCluggage introduced Hank Aaron by quoting him: "I had to break that record. I had to do it for Jackie and my people and myself and for everybody who ever called me nigger."

Aaron was doing it, of course, for Jackie Robinson. Hank Aaron broke Babe Ruth's record of 714 home runs with 755 of them from 1954 to 1976. He hit safely nearly three times as much (3,771) as he struck out (1,383), retiring with a .305 lifetime batting average.

It was Cardinal pitcher Curt Simmons who famously said, "Trying to throw a fastball past Aaron is like trying to sneak the sunrise past a rooster."

Hank Aaron was the last player from the Negro Leagues to play Major League Baseball, first for the Milwaukee Braves, starting at age 20, then the Atlanta Braves and his last two years with the Milwaukee Brewers.

At 6 feet and 180 pounds, Aaron was by no means a wholly

intimidating figure. LA Dodger Stan Williams was, at 230 pounds, 6-feet 5-inches tall with a blistering fastball and a nickname: "The Big Hurt." One day he hit Aaron in the helmet so hard the ball "bounced up into the press box," according to center fielder Duke Snider. First baseman Gil Hodges urged Aaron to "go get him."

Aaron didn't. He waited. "My mama didn't raise no fools," he said. The next time up he hit a Williams' pitch out of the park. Williams had tried to apologize, but Aaron would have none of it.

"The thing I had on my side was patience. It's something you pick up pretty naturally when you grow up Black in Alabama. When you wait all your life for respect and equality and a seat in the front of the bus, it's nothing to wait a little while for the slider inside," Aaron said after the game.

More than 350 people attended the dinner that year at the Mashantucket Pequot Casino. Aaron sat with Jim Rice on his right and Gaylord Perry on his left. Also there were Buck Showalter, Gene Michael, Tommy Harper, Bob Montgomery and George Scott, who said he idolized Aaron.

"I was a teammate of Hank's in Milwaukee. Hank Aaron was the best offensive player in the history of baseball. Ted Williams was the best hitter of all time, but Hank was the best offensive player in the history of the game – all the way around . . . Hank Aaron was devastating," said Scott.

Aaron went up to bat 12,364 times from 1954 to 1976 and retired holding several records: 2,297 RBI, 1,477 extra base hits, 6,856 total bases.

How do you top Hank Aaron? Maybe with his teammate

Joe Torre, a headliner at the next dinner in 1997.

Joe and Hank were teammates from 1960 to 1968, which includes when the Braves moved from Milwaukee to Atlanta. In fact in their first game in Atlanta, April 12, 1966, a total of 50,671 fans saw Torre smack two homers. He hit 36 that year. Aaron hit 44.

Thirty years later Joe Torre managed the New York Yankees to a World Series Championship. They defeated Atlanta. A few months later at the foundation dinner in January, Joe was having his picture taken with a young boy. Joe was seated, pulled the boy onto his right knee and asked him his name.

"Michael," answered the boy.

"Nice to meet you Michael," Torre said, "My name is Joe."

The boy's eyes grew wide. "I know," he said, as reported on site by Vickie Fulkerson of The Day newspaper.

Jackie Robinson's widow, Rachel, was signing copies of "Jackie Robinson, An Intimate Portrait" written by her for the 50th anniversary of breaking the color barrier in major league baseball. Sales were brisk.

Dan Adams was 3-years-old when John Ellis signed with the Yankees.

Now he owned Adams Wealth Management and Joe Stellato asked him to join the foundation board and put him in charge of that 1997 dinner.

"Then John called me the next morning and told me that Zimmer, Stottlemyre and Torre cancelled. I said 'don't worry we'll figure something out.'

'Then John said, 'You passed the test. They're coming.'

"What a joker! But he's so dedicated," said Adams.

He echoes Mohegan Maynard Strickland who said, "John is a great host – smile on his face – he makes it all work - the ambassador. Jane is serious, a hard worker. John has that personality – he could sell you the New London bridge."

For 22 years after incorporating in 1987, the foundation's President and Executive Director Jane Ellis didn't take a salary.

As chair of the 1997 dinner, Adams had a tables committee, a program committee – "we sold ads for the first time" – an auction committee.

"We had bi-weekly then weekly meetings as it got closer to the dinner. We came up with trinket prizes – a dozen golf balls, an umbrella if you sold a table. These guys got a charge out of getting 12 golf balls," said Adams.

It was $2,500 a table in 1997. The first dinner was $100. "Imagine paying $100 to be with Mickey Mantle and Whitey Ford!" he said.

He was getting excited talking about how they put together that dinner more than 20 years earlier. "My daughter Rachel, was 17, she made and sold bracelets at the dinner, life rings. My two youngest sons Matthew and Dan Jr., they worked, wrapping gifts, setting up, they loved being close to the players but they never forgot they were involved with helping people who are struggling."

"It was a fun atmosphere and you felt good about doing it. And you had a good time doing it. It became a cause," he said; and of course it was.

Adams was echoed by another board member, newspaper Editor and Publisher Eliot C. White: "John Ellis is one of those few larger than life people that I have met in life. His big presence with big ideas made him such a positive force for the huge success CCF."

White, of the Meriden Record-Journal, rose to vice president of the foundation board.

"Occasionally John would have an idea for the board that was a bit far fetched. Jane was always there to skillfully rein him in without a confrontation. It is so admirable that their joint focus has been so successful in helping cancer victims. As a lifetime Yankee fan and a cancer survivor, it was personally rewarding to watch the success of CCF," said White.

Adams found that Ellis, "has a very fertile mind, and a lot of courage. He's strong physically and mentally. If he wants to do something, he'll get there. He's the toughest man I ever met.

"He has a keen eye, a sharp biz guy, an unbelievable networker, he knows people in all walks of life, knows how to gain access."

Adams pushed the idea of an endowment for the foundation and helped the Ellises set it up. At 4 or 5 percent, they let it grow, half for cancer, half for the endowment. Within five years there was $1 million, "now there's $10 million," said Adams.

"At the foundation we called in our friends," said Ellis. "When you need them they gotta be there. Life is trust your friend."

Chapter 16
Ten Years In

At the 10th anniversary dinner in 1998 Carl Yastrzemski didn't sit at the head table with Don Zimmer, Bob Watson, Walt Hriniak, Bob Schaefer and Sammy Ellis. The Triple Crown winner in 1967 with a .324 batting average, 44 home runs and 121 runs batted in, and the recipient of the Most Valuable Player Award that year, Yaz wanted to be out on the floor with the dinner guests.

"He told me he'd sit at a small table in the back of the room and sign programs for as long as it took to get everyone's program signed," remembers the emcee that night, newspaper Editor and Publisher Reid MacCluggage. "Yaz was eager to mix with the guests."

The headline in his newspaper, The Day of New London, read: "Loyalty between Yaz and fans remains strong."

He was the first American Leaguer to have 3,000 hits and 400 home runs. He was inducted into the Hall of Fame in 1989.

That year Don Zimmer was named the National League Manager of the Year, leading the Chicago Cubs to a 93-69 season, National League Eastern Division champions. Zim told the foundation audience that winning the division was "like the difference between .299 and .300. You'd think it was 50 points higher than .299."

Zimmer came back to the dinners for the next 14 years.

In 2001 Adams told those in attendance, "We expect to allocate approximately $200,000 to our fund to help families and more than $100,000 toward cancer research at Sloan Kettering from tonight's dinner. This truly is a testament to all of you and your commitment to help those who are suffering."

It was the year the foundation brought in sports casters to host the Q&As with the players. First was Suzyn Waldman, the former Broadway actress ("Man of la Mancha") and breast cancer survivor. Hers was the first voice heard on the pioneering all-sports radio station WFAN when it debuted in 1987.

Waldman made sports history in January 1999 as the person who brought the feuding Yogi Berra and George Steinbrenner back together. It was on her WFAN show that the two reconciled after a 14-year rift. Steinbrenner had fired Berra as Yankees manager in 1985 after only 16 games.

Now she was before a live dinner audience jousting with David Justice, Jay Payton, Mookie Wilson, Don Zimmer, Brook Fordyce and Dave Campo. The next two years it was with Zimmer, Fordyce, Roger Clemens, Mel Stottlemyre, Mariano Rivera, David Wells, Pete Walker, Gene Michael, Moose Skowron and Hank Bauer.

Longtime roommates Skowron and Bauer, with Stottlemeyer

and Zimmer, were back in 2004 with Jason Giambi, Jeremy Giambi, Johnny Damon and Whitey Ford when Waldman's Yankees broadcasting partner John "It is high, it is far, it is gone!" Sterling handled the dinner.

"They were both great!" said Jane Ellis. "It was very kind and generous of them to support us and participate," she said of Waldman and Sterling.

A table of 10 went for $10,000, often paid by the diners' corporation.

This year Whitey Ford offered himself up as an auction item. Win the bidding, get your picture taken with the Chairman of the Board. It began at $300, $400, $500, then $1,000. Whitey was smiling that broad smile of his. Johnny Damon, then of the Red Sox, was bidding against a guy who was there with his $2,500 end-of-year bonus.

It was up to $1,500 but Damon took it to $1,750. His bid was met. The duo went back and forth across the ballroom. Damon kept smiling at his bidding war opponent. $2,000, then $2,100, and then $2,400. The man with the small bonus stood up, in an across-the-room pleading to Damon, his palms outstretched, bid $2,500. Damon gave him a little wave.

Then the winning bidder was shaking hands with Whitey Ford and introducing the Hall of Fame pitcher to his boss's daughter. She got Whitey's jersey and put it on for the photo.

"Whitey," the guy asked, "did you ever shake off Yogi on his called pitches?"

"Nah, Yogi was too smart," said Whitey with a big grin.

As we have seen, Mrs. Lou Gehrig saw something in the young John Ellis. It's a wonder she didn't notice Whitey's teammate Bill "Moose" Skowron, who lorded over first base for the Yankees in the 1950s and '60s, and whose fielding average edged out Lou Gehrig's .992 to .991. Moose came to the 2003 dinner.

He didn't have the offensive stats of the Iron Horse, but in 1961, the year Mantle chased Maris for the home run record, Skowron hit one out every other time Mantle did. Mantle: 54 homers, Skowron: 28 homers, Maris: 61 homers, breaking Ruth's record. The M&M boys going after Ruth's record held the nation in awe.

Those years when the1950s turned to the 1960s, the first Black man on the Yankees, Elston Howard, moved elegantly behind the plate as Yogi Berra segued to left field ("It gets late out there early.") Bobby Richardson replaced scrappy Gil Mc-Dougald at second. Whitey Ford presided on the mound. Clete Boyer and Tony Kubek held down the left side of the infield. Moose Skowron was the mainstay on first and, of course, Mantle and Maris in center and right.

There was something about the Moose. Maybe he was getting overlooked - this big guy who hit .375 in the 1960 World Series. "I don't always swing at strikes. I swing at the ball when it looks big," he told the Sporting News earlier that year. Whatever his eyes saw traveling at him at 90 mph, it worked. He led the team in hitting that year at .309. His Yankees pay was $22,500.

"There was just one Moose, he was out of the mold," his manager Ralph Houk remembered in his book "Season of Glory." "He was a quiet, hardworking guy who would do anything for anybody . . . He never complained . . . everybody kidded him because he took everything so serious," wrote Houk. "He was always in the ballgame. He'd get it done. He hit the ball hard (and) was an above-average fielder, though not too many people noticed that," he wrote.

Moose was in a sport coat and tie, signing baseballs at the 2003 foundation dinner. He was 72, but still had that crew cut and that handsome, chiseled face. The crowds swelled around David Wells and Mariano Rivera, but it was a steady line to Moose Skowron signing baseballs. He was excited and smiled and talked to 12-year-old boys who must have thought this guy was ancient.

As dinner was about to be served inside the large ballroom, the players waited to be introduced. Eighty-year-old Hank Bauer strode into the room and up onto the stage to healthy applause.

Next came Moose, who attended six dinners between 2003 and 2011. As he listened this night to the rousing introduction "he hit over .300 five years ... 14 years in the majors ... ladies and gentleman, Moose Skowron" - it was like he lit up. His face beamed, his broad shoulders pulled his large frame into the room. He pumped both arms, clenched both fists, and with a fervor reserved for those who remember, he hollered as much to himself as to us: "Yes!" Then Moose Skowron broke into a run. At least half of the 800 diners stood in adulation and applause as he joined his former teammate and roommate Bauer, waving back at the crowd. Together they slammed 323 home runs for the Yankees.

Moose Skowron played in 1,658 major league baseball games, accumulating 1,566 hits, 407 of them for extra bases, including 211 home runs, 888 RBI and a lifetime .282 batting average (Maris's was .260). In a poignant irony of baseball trades - Skowron hit .385 helping the Los Angeles Dodgers beat the Yankees 4-0 in the 1963 World Series.

Ellis broke into the majors in 1969, two years after William Joseph Skowron retired. Moose said he was honored to come and help the foundation do its important work. Seeing him again, still so revved up, reminded the soul about lasting passion.

Moose and Hank came back for several more years. They joked about how on the baseball card circuit and at fantasy camps they roomed together "in case one of us dies."

But they left this world separately. Cancer took Hank Bauer at 84 in 2007. Moose was with him in the hospital a few days before he died. Five years later, at 81, hit with cancer too, it was congestive heart failure that got Moose Skowron.

Bauer's last foundation dinner in 2007 was the first dinner to raise a million dollars. Besides Hank and Moose, it featured David Cone, David Wells, Don Larsen, Yogi Berra, Joe Girardi, Jim Leyland, Don Zimmer, Mel Stottlemyre, Brian McRae, Barry Lyons, Ron Darling, John Franco, and Keith Hernandez. Cone, 44 at the time, was honored that night, the foundation's 20th anniversary dinner at the Mohegan Sun. A top pitcher with the Mets, Yankees, Blue Jays and Royals, after a 4-14 season with the Yankees in 2000, he refused to retire, pitched for the Red Sox in 2001, and after a year of retirement, came back in '03 with the Mets.

With a 194-126 career record, "This time of year, with pitchers and catchers reporting, I still get the itch," he said. "It's tough. What am I going to do? I'm a baseball player. That's all I know. You don't have any practical experience in the real world, and you panic. . . 'How's my arm feel?' I miss being good at it."

Wells, Cone's longtime teammate and close friend, nodded and smiled. He intended to retire after last season, but couldn't bring himself to do it. He signed a one-year contract with the Padres, his career record at 230-148.

"I should quit lying to you guys and just admit that I'm going to go until they kick me out," said Wells, who would turn 44 that May. "After last season, I was 99 percent sure I was going to retire. But I spend some time hunting and I start thinking, 'What am I going to do?' I could play golf, but that must get tired after a while. All my friends work, so I'd be by myself. Finally, I asked my wife, 'Is it OK if I play again?'"

Chapter 17
Don Zimmer R.I.P

Don Zimmer was married on a baseball diamond, spent 66 years in the game as a player, coach, manager and adviser. He died at 83 in June 2014. He had become a mainstay of support for the foundation. This is the speech John Ellis gave about "Zim" at the 2015 Foundation dinner.

He may not have uttered every word, but we present it here in full:

When we lost Don Zimmer in June, we lost one of the greats – a great family man, a great baseball man, a great friend of the foundation.

But true legends never die, and Zim will always be remembered at the foundation for the 20 years he came to these celebrity dinners to raise funds for needy cancer patients.

Twenty years. He holds the record.

He could have stayed in sunny Florida where he lived, but he came here instead in the middle of winter, often fighting through pain until he just couldn't do it anymore.

Zim stood up for the foundation because he was a stand-up guy.

Don Zimmer R.I.P

And so, Zim, on behalf of the foundation and the many people you've helped, we say thank you. The Connecticut Sports Foundation would not be where it is today without you. You were our heart and soul, our spirit through those years, and we honor you tonight.

His beloved wife Soot was here by his side every one of those years, and tonight Soot and the Zimmer family are with us – son Tom and his wife Marion, daughter Donna and her husband Pudge and grandson Beau. They're here to help us pay tribute to Don and his unwavering dedication to the Foundation and the cause of fighting cancer.

There was no greater fan of the Connecticut Sports Foundation than Don Zimmer – a man whose 66-year career in baseball might never have happened if not for his grit and fighting spirit. He was beaned so badly in a minor league game at the beginning of his career that he lay unconscious for 13 days. Doctors said he'd never play again . . . but he did.

Zim was a fighter.

First time I ever met him was in the 1970s at the bottom of a bench-clearing brawl between the Red Sox and the Indians. I was playing first base for the Indians and Zim was coaching third for the Sox. There he was with his huge Popeye forearms swinging away and there I was holding him in a headlock.

Zim was a fighter.

Ten years later – it's 1982 now – he becomes the manager of the Texas Rangers where I was winding up a 13-year career. We were all excited about playing for a players' manager, and I'd had a great spring, so when he called me into his office I figured he was going to tell me how valuable I was to the team. We were going to have a great year.

I get there, he says, "You stink!"

"You are the worst ballplayer I've ever seen. The team is releasing you."

When Zim put the stink on you, it stuck.

123

I go from there to being the advance scout for him, but the season's going downhill fast. We're in last place. I figure it couldn't be my scouting. Then one day Zim calls me in. "John," he says, "I want to release three players and replace them with some minor leaguers. These guys stink." I knew it couldn't have been my scouting.

I said, "Are you sure?"

So a meeting's called in Chicago with the owner Eddie Chiles and general manager Eddie Robinson. And Zimmer says, "Gentlemen, we're here to improve the team by releasing three guys and bringing up some minor leaguers." And Eddie Chiles says, "That'll cost me three million!"

There we were. Zimmer on one side, the owner on the other (a familiar place for Don) and me in the middle.

So Robinson goes around the room. What do you think? What do you think? Zimmer says, "They stink." He gets to me. I'm thinking, do I go with Chiles and save my executive baseball career or do I go with Zimmer.

"They stink," I said.

Well, we lost the next 13 games and Chiles fires Don, then me. In one very short season I'd been fired twice. My baseball career was over.

But not Zim's.

He'd already played alongside Jackie Robinson and Pee Wee Reese, helped win the only World Series the Dodgers ever won in Brooklyn, and, by 1982, had managed San Diego, Boston and Texas. He was at Yankee Stadium for Don Larsen's perfect game, at Fenway coaching third for Boston when Carlton Fisk hit that dramatic home run in the sixth game of the '75 World Series, and at Fenway again for Bucky Dent's famous homer.

Enough great baseball experience for a lifetime.

But Zim wasn't done. He went on to manage the Cubs, guiding them in '89 to first in the National League East, winning NL manager of the year, and giving Joe Girardi his first big major league break.

And then he joined Joe Torre's Yankees as bench coach, helping to guide young players to greatness. Derek Jeter, Bernie Williams, Jorge Posada, Mariano Rivera and Andy Pettitte – players that Gene Michael had brought along in the minors over the years and Buck Showalter had prepared after bringing up Jeter, Posada, Rivera and Pettitte in '95, Buck's last year as Yankees manager. By 1996 they were ready, and under Torre and Zimmer they won four world championships.

Marty Noble wrote that Zim wore the caps of 18 franchises in his six decades in the game – 13 in the big leagues . . . and one army helmet.

What a career.

But Zim was more than baseball. He was devoted to his beloved Soot, their children and grandchildren. He was loyal to friends and true to his word. He stood up for what was right.

In 1978 when he was managing the Red Sox he got wind that Bob Ryan, the Boston Globe writer, was going to Butte, Montana to see Zim's son Tom, then an Independent League manager. "He called me over right behind home plate at Fenway," Ryan said, "pressed a $50 bill into my hand and said, 'You take Tom and Marion out to dinner.'" That paid for three steak dinners in Butte in those days.

Family man, baseball man . . . friend.

That was Don Zimmer.

Chapter 18
'Welcome to our Mohegan homeland'

Chief Mutawi Mutahash (Many Hearts) Marilynn Malerba, the 18th chief of the Mohegan tribe and the first female chief, gave the blessing, first in Mohegan and then in English, at the 2017 foundation dinner.

Chief for seven years into the life-time appointment, she took the microphone and said, "It is traditional during the blessing that anyone able to stand, please do." As the hundreds of paying guests rose in the cavernous Uncas Ballroom, she said, "Thank you."

"Great spirit we thank you for this day and all the days to follow. We thank you for our friends who stand before us and for their safe journey. We welcome them to our Mohegan homeland."

In a calm, soothing voice, she asked her ancestors, "to guide us" in friendship and in sharing good food. "May the great spirit who is in all the world bless our families" and ensure "in the paths that we walk, may we all live in peace."

Along her path she earned a bachelor of nursing from the College of St. Joseph, a master's degree in public administration from the University of Connecticut, a Doctor of Nursing Practice from Yale, and served as the director of Cardiology and Pulmonary services at Lawrence and Memorial Hospital in New London. She is the great-granddaughter of Mohegan Chief Matagha and her mother, Loretta Roberge, served on the Tribal Council that built the Mohegan Sun Casino.

Chief Many Hearts was followed a bit later in the evening by David "Big Papi" Ortiz of the Boston Red Sox, who no one doubts will be inducted into the Baseball Hall of Fame his first year of eligibility in 2022.

He hit .455 in the three World Series he played in and was asked how he did that.

"Either you do that or you go home is the only way I can explain it," said the veteran designated hitter and sometimes first baseman. "I'm from the Dominican Republic. I grew up doing that. Handling pressure is part of what we do growing up in the Dominican Republic," where, he said, "there was a shooting every day."

Twenty years after his rookie season in 1997 with Minnesota, he shared the stage with Steven Matz, 26, of the Mets who pitched in the World Series as a rookie; Tyler Austin, 25, then of the New York Yankees who, with teammate Aaron Judge, hit home runs in their first at bats. Austin survived testicular cancer as a teenager. And Luis Severino, 23, of the Yankees who would win 14 and lose only six that season.

127

Ortiz, with his 541 homers (17the on the all-time list ahead of Mickey Mantle with 536, behind Mike Schmidt with 548) was asked what advice he'd give these young players.

"We are in one of the best eras in baseball with young, talented players. I was 20 years old and I wasn't close to what these guys bring to the table, the way they want to get better. The fans know when you give everything you have. The fans appreciate that. We try our best, that's what I expect from young players."

Pause here for a big round of applause from the thousand guests at the foundation's 30th annual dinner.

They gave similar recognition to emcee Mike Francesa of Mike and the Mad Dog fame on WFAN radio in New York. He was the voice of the foundation dinners for 11 years, but was retiring from both the airwaves and the dinner circuit.

"Mike never accepted compensation," announced John Ellis. "He's the greatest sports radio broadcaster in the United States." Then Ellis gave him a big bear hug up at the podium and said, "I love you buddy." And an era ended.

The next year, 2018, it was Emmy Award-winning Michael ("see ya") Kay as emcee. He had some questions for special guest Derek Jeter. But the first thing he said upon taking the microphone was, "John Ellis has done remarkable work with the foundation. The promise he made has been kept. He and his wife Jane have done a remarkable job."

Then he turned to Jeter. "You could make the argument that Derek is the greatest shortstop in the history of baseball."

You could. But according to ESPN, he is 5th on the list of all-time greats behind 1. Honus Wagner, 2. Alex Rodriguez, 3.

Ernie Banks, and 4. Cal Ripken Jr.

No matter, Kay had a portrait of the Yankee captain at bat up on stage and held an auction – hauling in $15,000 for the cause.

So, Derek, do you miss playing, retiring in 2014 after 20 years? Jeter looked surprised by the question, but said quietly into the microphone that he doesn't miss playing. "I was tired. . . I gave it everything I had. Mentally, I was ready to hang it up."

"What was your best moment?

"I don't know. Obviously the five times we won (the World Series) . . . That's what you play for. To win," he said.

He sunk a reported $25 million (he made $266 million as a player) as a 2-percent partner of the Miami Marlins, where he is CEO. "Own a team, something I've always wanted to do" – and he wants to make them winners.

Chapter 19
'We will be the greatest charity'

John Ellis is not necessarily a reflective fellow. But when he starts to think about things, he usually expresses them through a competitive lens.

"We will be the greatest charity in Connecticut!" he proclaimed one day. He paused. "Maybe not in my lifetime," said the 72-year-old.

Well, maybe, for a foundation like his and Jane's. According to the State of Connecticut, the Connecticut Cancer Foundation of Old Saybrook had in 2019 total assets of $10,458, 301. By way of comparison, the Make-a-Wish Foundation of Trumbull, serving children with critical illnesses, had $7,000,647. The Terri Brodeur Breast Cancer Foundation of New London had $878,465. Project Genesis, Inc. of Willimantic serves people with a spectrum of disabilities, $8,240,182. Ditto Outreach Inc. of Newington, $9,660,206.

Many Major League baseball players have established foundations. Here are a few:

The David Ortiz Children's Fund supports kids with heart ailments in New England and the Dominican Republic. In 2018 its total assets were $1,744,549.

The Cal Ripken Sr. Foundation in 2018 had assets of $29,783,624. Through at-risk youth programs and "Youth Development Parks," it served 1.5 million kids in the U.S. in 2019 "developing life skills, building character, connecting kids positively with local law enforcement, and teaching how to make productive choices for their future."

Derek Jeter's Turn2 Foundation since its launch in 1996 has awarded more than $30 million through programs to motivate young people to turn away from drugs and alcohol.

Former New York Met Tug McGraw was diagnosed with a brain tumor in 2003. He established The Tug McGraw Foundation to help people diagnosed with debilitating neurological brain conditions such as brain tumors, traumatic brain injury, and post-traumatic stress disorder. He died in 2004 but his foundation lived on, receiving $1,727,595 in gifts from 2014-2018.

The Connecticut Cancer Foundation strategy has always been rooted in sports, particularly baseball.

"Sometimes we raised more than a million dollars in a night," said Mohegan Tribal official Maynard Strickland. Ellis punctuates Strickland's statement: "A One Million Dollar Dinner! I'm talking net."

In 2019 the foundation provided almost half a million dollars in grants to 626 individuals and families. The 2020 dinner, with more than 900 guests, raised more than $600,000. In its 33 years so far, the foundation has provided more than $6.4

million to more than 7,700 cancer patients, and has given more than $2.4 million for cancer research at Memorial Sloan Kettering Cancer Center where Dr. Joachim Yahalom and his medical team saved John Ellis's life in 1986.

The Connecticut Cancer Foundation received a "Highly Rated" status, three out of four stars, from Charity Navigator, the nation's largest evaluator of charities. The foundation in 2019 received four stars, a perfect 100 for "accountability and transparency." Administrative costs made up only 13.6 percent of the annual budget. For the first 22 years Jane was unpaid. Her salary now is a modest $96,000.

Baseball stars aside, the Ellises realized they needed corporate support. John reached back to his Little League baseball days. One kid he played against was Leo Chupaska, who grew up to be the chief financial officer of the Mohegan Tribal Nation. As a major league baseball player, John met Maynard Strickland at his bar in Anaheim, California, the home of the California Angels. When his teams traveled to the West Coast, John would meet Maynard for dinner, forging a life-long friendship with the man who eventually would be in charge of sports at the Mohegan Sun casino.

Chupaska and Strickland introduced the Ellises to Mitchell Grossinger Etess, chief executive officer of the Mohegan Tribal Gaming Authority, and member of the famous Grossinger family of Catskills hospitality.

A partnership was forged and has lasted for more than 17 years. The Connecticut Cancer Foundation has a private contract with the Mohegan Tribal Nation. It provides for players' speaking fees, their hotel rooms, food and beverages, and other goods and services in kind, adding up to six figures each year.

Players and dinner guests "gamble too. It works out both ways," Strickland said. And a lot of the players, "guys like Joe Girardi, they put the money right back in with the auctions," he said.

The tribal nation is "committed to defeating cancer," said John. The tribe's "willingness and ability to help their community, as well as helping Connecticut's neediest cancer patients is a testament to its corporate social responsibility. We are so grateful for their support. Without it the foundation would not have been so successful. The Mohegan Sun's connections with WFAN and Mike Francesa, ESPN and YES Network's Michael Kay and the Yankees have had tremendous and effective results for our cancer patients who need us now more than ever. These partners have made the world a better place and made Connecticut's cancer patients' financial burden a little easier," said John.

Both John and Jane emphasize how the work of the foundation is a team effort. But when founding board member Vince Genovese died of lung cancer in 2008, John took note that "the foundation would not be where it is today without his charity and his involvement."

John was a Texas Ranger when he met Genovese. They were roommates in Texas for six years and became "more like brothers than friends . . . He became my best friend for over 30 years and was my best man when Jane and I were married," said John. "I never laughed as much as when Vince and I were together."

After he retired from baseball and went into real estate full time, he sold Vince's Powr-Flite floor care equipment company for more than $20 million. "His personal trust in me is something that I have never before experienced and never will," John said in his eulogy at Vince's funeral.

"Socrates said, 'Be of good cheer about death and know this as a truth -- that no evil can happen to a good man, either in life or after death.' Vince has no concerns," said John.

Vince's daughter Karol, through the Vincent Genovese Memorial Foundation, donated $250,000 to build the museum and hall of fame in the new foundation office building in Old Saybrook. "Karol's gift made it possible for the foundation to be available to the community to engage parents and children to learn about our rich history, the importance of charitable giving, and the power of unconditional kindness," said John.

There have been fewer kids at the dinners in recent years, as players begged off signing baseballs. Ticket prices increased to raise more funds for cancer patients, and attendance sometimes rose to more than 1,000 guests, making it nearly impossible to ask for autographs. But children remain central to the purpose of the foundation. Beyond the contributions to children and families hit with cancer, the foundation's building itself is a shrine.

Walk in the entrance to the Hall of Fame Sports Memorabilia Museum with its giant-size photographs of baseball immortals at play. Listen to the lyricism in this philanthropist who once had a signed catcher's mitt issued by Spalding Sporting Goods, Inc.:

America was the land of opportunity where even a poor boy could grow up to be Babe Ruth. It means your hero taking the time to tell you to never stop believing in yourself. Opportunity means sometimes your best is better than mine, but we will meet again. Opportunity is the selfless act in sacrificing your momentary chance at glory for the good of the team. It means an 8-year-old boy sleeping with his mitt on just in case a late-night game breaks out in his dreams. It means closing your eyes and swinging as hard as you can. It means hope springing eternal and waiting for next year, again, and again, and again. What does baseball mean to me? In a word: Everything.

John is on a roll here.

Our position at the Foundation is that kids are part of our future. Jane's Hall of Fame creates self-esteem, shows how sports can impact our communities, that leadership is helping others and following your own convictions. We believe that by offering children a visit to our Hall of Fame with audio storytelling that links the visual masterpieces will nourish leadership qualities in children.

Our Hall of Fame will remind the public how sports are an integral part of our country's national memory, and celebrates the Major League ballplayers who came to our dinners and raised funds for thousands of cancer patients. Our Hall of Fame and museum will engage parents and children using its rich history and background to teach the importance of charitable giving, the power of unconditional kindness and leadership, and the value and significance of baseball.

Jane's office is literally around the corner from their hall of fame in the foundation building, a handsome one-story white colonial structure at 15 North Main Street at the corner with Rt. 1, the Post Road in Old Saybrook, Connecticut.

"John's the ambassador, everybody loves John. Jane does all the hard work. John was a tough guy in baseball and Jane can be tougher," said Maynard Strickland.

135

Chapter 20
The Mission

Brittney Blye's 2 1/2- year- old daughter, Livinia, was diagnosed with a stage three, rare childhood kidney cancer called
Wilms Tumor. The seven-inch tumor and her left kidney were
removed in a 13-hour emergency surgery followed by 11 consecutive cycles of radiation and 33 weeks of chemotherapy.

"You can't even think straight. Nothing else mattered, but
getting Liv better," said her mother.

Add in her middle name and Livinia Vaune became something of a mantra: "Liv-Vaune" had the ring "Live-On." Brittney is a Kundalini yoga teacher and Liv is a part of that
Dharma, given the spiritual name, "Rakha," which means spiritual protection.

"I always felt that Liv was divinely protected," her mother
said.

Brittney is a single mother and while caring for Liv during
her treatment a hospital social worker told her that the Connecticut Cancer Foundation would like to help. "To feel sup-

ported at a time like this was invaluable," she said. Liv is happy, healthy and nearly six years in remission heading into fourth grade.

Brittney serves on the foundation's Cycle Against Cancer committee and formed a cycle team in 2015, the same year her daughter was the foundation's "ambassador." She was "Li-Vaune-RakhaN" (Live On - Rock on) for the cycle against cancer in Old Saybrook.

"We do Cycles Against Cancer every year," at cycle centers around the state raising significant contributions, she said. For example, Joe Fay and Kati Papoosha, owners of Iron House Fitness in Old Saybrook, have raised more than a quarter of a million dollars since 2016.

Foundation donations to families can be up to $2,000. For chosen ambassadors, selected by oncology social workers, at foundation events, it can be much more. Brittney was "astonished" to receive "thousands and thousands," for Livinia's treatment.

"I hope my daughter's story offers hope and courage and awareness that you can come out on the other side of cancer. The foundation created a sense of unity and a tribe of support. Jane is a rock-star and one of my heroes because she truly cares about helping people," said Brittney. "Fundraising each year has given this tragic experience a purpose -- we can now help others."

The Connecticut Cancer Foundation hosts an elegant and expansive Web site, www.ctcancerfoundation.org that banners the phrase "It all Started with a Promise," a reference to the 38-year-old John Ellis's pledge to God "you let me live, I'll help everybody I can."

And he has. The web site displays detailed financials, dozens of photos from the annual dinners and other events, and heart-rending stories of the people the foundation has supported.

Kyle Ashley

The star of his soccer team, Kyle Ashley was just six years old when he was diagnosed with bone cancer in 2017. He underwent surgery and chemo to fight the cancer, a grueling experience for anyone, but he never lost his smile or gave up. Even at such a young age, Kyle was incredibly thoughtful and kind. The bravery of pediatric cancer patients will take your breath away and Kyle was one of the bravest - his courage was an inspiration . . .

Kyle was the Ambassador for the 2018 M.e.l.t.-a-thon Against Cancer and his entire community turned out to participate that year in support. Teachers, friends, family - everyone came. Kyle had such a great time -the whole day, he had a great, big smile on his face!

We were all heartbroken when Kyle passed away on December 18, 2018 after the cancer spread to his lungs. His legacy of kindness lives on - every year on his birthday, September 3, people are encouraged to do a random act of kindness in his memory.

Brynn Levitsky

On Friday, Octrber 19, 2012, Brynn Levitsky's life took a drastic change in course. At 22 months old, she was running around, playing with her dog, swinging on her swing set and living life to the fullest. However, on that rainy Friday, Brynn was not acting like herself. A few weeks earlier, her Mom, Kara, noticed that she was unusually sleepy and running a low-grade fever. Her doctor attributed it to teething, but when Brynn began re-fusing to walk, Kara called the doctor and insisted that she be seen for the second time that week . . . Later that evening, Brynn was diagnosed with Acute Myeloid Leukemia.

Brynn completed four intense rounds of chemotherapy and at the end of her treatment, tests showed she was in remission. Unfortunately, after 20 months of thriving as a healthy and happy 3-year-old, Brynn relapsed in May 2014 and needed a bone marrow transplant. She spent a year in isolation to recover. In March 2015 she was healthy and could not wait to start kindergarten. However in September 2015 she relapsed once again despite her being healthy, active and happy. She began fighting this battle again for the third time. In 2018 Brynn lost her long battle with cancer.

Nate Rosario

Like most kids his age, Nate Rosario loves soccer, Star Wars, and playing video games with his friends. Unfortunately, Nate was diagnosed with leukemia in July 2017 and immediately began a regimen of chemotherapy that included countless tests, medical procedures, and trips to the hospital. As his primary caregiver, his mother, Damaris, was unable to work and had to surrender her car, leaving her with no way to get to and from the hospital. Nate was the Ambassador for the Cycle Against Cancer at New York Sports Club in 2017 and CCF was able to greatly aid Nate and his family, helping them acquire a car and assisting with other living expenses. Nate turned 17 in September 2020.

The annual dinner is the big source of funds for the foundation, but Jane and John don't stop there.

Why not Fishing Against Cancer? The 2017 Brewer Pilots Point/Sea Tow Fishing tournament had men hauling in huge stripers and bluefish and $24,000.

The 2017 Enterprise Builders (of Newington) Golf Tournament at the Lake of Isles Golf Resort at Foxwoods Casino brought out 160 golfers to benefit Connecticut military veterans struck by cancer. The 2019 tourney featured former major leaguers Bobby Valentine and Roy White. It provided a $10,000 donation to the family of the tournament "ambassador," Zabdiel Sarabia, a child from Norwalk battling leukemia.

From 2016 to 2019 the foundation provided more than $1,760,000 to families and $490,000 in research grants. The annual dinners have been the mainstay, but the indoor cycling events have been a significant source of funds. In each gym each team of four raises $1,000 or more. In 2018, for example, Iron House Fitness in Old Saybrook hosted more than 90 spinners raising more than $42,000. Statewide, cycling against cancer raised $146,675 that year.

"They have become very successful and we are grateful to everyone involved," Jane said.

A bigger potential for fund raising is police officers growing beards/mustaches. The small town of Ledyard's police department held a "No Shave November" fundraiser in 2017 and donated $1,750 to the foundation.

The idea took off and soon there were bearded cops everywhere in November. In two years some 60 police and college campus security departments raised more than $200,000 for cancer patients by donating the money saved on shaving products and asking for donations from the community.

In 2020 Schick Edgewell Personal Care through its brands Schick Hydro and Schick Extreme signed on to sponsor the No Shave November event and Jane set a fundraising goal of $500,000.

Chapter 21
The 2020 Dinner

At the 2020 dinner a painting by Connecticut artist Patrick Ganino of that night's headliner, Gary Sanchez, stood out at the silent auction. Sanchez stands tall, his full 6' 2", mask pushed up to the top of his head, his hand resting on his chest protector. You wonder what he's thinking.

The asking price was $750. Later that night a boy and his father were gingerly carrying it around.

A framed Yogi Berra collage was priced at $350; a Tom Brady signed football for $1,350; a signed Kobe Bryant (who had died in a helicopter crash two weeks earlier) basketball for $4,900; Derek Jeter at bat, $1,800; Marilyn Monroe and Bruce Springsteen portraits for $375 each – long tables filled with memorabilia, always bring in big bucks for the cause.

The live auction does even better with dinner guests bidding against one another. Four Red Sox tickets with on-field privileges during batting practice and an overnight in Boston sold for $3,500. A spring training game with overnight and private meet-and-greet with Sanchez and other Yankees sold for $5,000. The asking price was $10,000 for an overnight at Mystic's Spicer Mansion for eight couples with dinner and "European breakfast." A bidding war got it up to $5,000 when the auctioneer offered it to both bidders – total $10,000 -- and the well-dressed dining crowd erupted in applause.

Then came the no-dry-eyes moment when the beautiful, brown-eyed Jane Ellis ascended to the microphone. She acknowledged that she rarely did this, usually leaving the speaking to her husband.

"I was compelled to get up tonight to share a story with you that broke my heart a couple of weeks ago. I met Evan. He's six years old battling a brain tumor. He was sitting there in a wheel chair, hooked up to oxygen . . . The overwhelmingly sad image of him struggling, so sweetly and intently, determined to bring a little piece of cake to his mouth has stuck with me since. I have seen a lot of cancer patients in my 33 years of doing this, but I was overcome with sorrow at seeing this little boy so unfairly struggling to do something that we all take so for granted and to witness his will to live! I can't get it out of my mind. Can we even begin to imagine what he has been through? John and I walked away in tears with a renewed determination to urge donors to help."

Evan's portrait was on the big wall screens. Jane asked everyone to take out their cellphones and click on the link they all just received.

"If everyone gives $100 or $50 or whatever you can do," she said, those donations would appear on the screens. "Our goal is

$25,000."

The screens instantly lit up with donation piling on donations. Within 10 minutes she had raised the $25,000.

"Thank you," she said.

John rejoined, "The need in Connecticut is greater than ever. We cannot do it alone. Please give your unconditional support." The Sanchez dinner raised more than $600,000.

"It has been a privilege. It has been our life," said Jane.

The End

Appendix

John Ellis

Positions: First Baseman and Catcher
Bats: Right • **Throws:** Right
6-2, 225lb (188cm, 102kg)
Born: August 21, 1948 (Age: 69-050d) in New London, CT

SUMMARY	WAR	AB	R	H	BA	HR	RBI	SB	OBP	SLG	OPS	OPS+
Career	3.0	2672	259	699	.262	69	391	6	.312	.392	.704	99

Standard Batting Show Minors   Share & more ▾   Glossary

Year	Age	Tm	Lg	G	PA	AB	R	H	2B	3B	HR	RBI	SB	CS	BB	SO	BA	OBP	SLG	OPS	OPS+	TB	GDP	HBP	SH	SF	IBB	Pos
1969	20	NYY	AL	22	65	62	2	18	4	0	1	8	0	2	1	11	.290	.308	.403	.711	101	25	0	1	0	1	0	2
1970	21	NYY	AL	78	249	226	24	56	12	1	7	29	0	1	18	47	.248	.305	.403	.708	98	91	5	2	0	3	0	3/S2
1971	22	NYY	AL	83	271	238	16	58	12	1	3	34	0	0	23	42	.244	.322	.340	.663	93	81	12	6	1	3	5	3/2
1972	23	NYY	AL	52	144	136	13	40	5	1	5	25	0	0	8	22	.294	.333	.456	.789	137	62	9	0	0	0	0	2/3
1973	24	CLE	AL	127	494	437	59	118	12	2	14	68	0	0	46	57	.270	.339	.403	.741	107	176	13	3	1	7	2	2D3
1974	25	CLE	AL	128	513	477	58	136	23	6	10	64	1	2	32	53	.285	.330	.421	.751	117	201	16	1	1	2	3	32D
1975	26	CLE	AL	92	316	296	22	68	11	1	7	32	0	1	14	33	.230	.266	.345	.610	73	102	13	2	0	4	2	2/D3
1976	27	TEX	AL	11	31	31	4	13	2	0	1	8	0	0	0	4	.419	.419	.581	1.000	189	18	1	0	0	0	0	/2D
1977	28	TEX	AL	49	127	119	7	28	7	0	4	15	0	0	8	26	.235	.283	.395	.678	83	47	1	0	0	0	2	2D/3
1978	29	TEX	AL	34	104	94	7	23	4	0	3	17	0	1	6	20	.245	.282	.383	.665	86	36	0	0	1	3	0	2/D
1979	30	TEX	AL	111	337	316	33	90	12	0	12	61	2	2	15	55	.285	.318	.437	.754	104	138	3	2	0	4	1	D3/2
1980	31	TEX	AL	73	200	182	12	43	9	1	1	23	3	0	14	23	.236	.290	.313	.603	69	57	6	1	0	3	1	3D/2
1981	32	TEX	AL	23	64	58	2	8	3	0	1	7	0	1	5	10	.138	.219	.241	.460	37	14	3	1	0	0	1	3/D
13 Yrs				883	2915	2672	259	699	116	13	69	391	6	10	190	403	.262	.312	.392	.704	99	1048	82	19	4	30	17	

Transactions

August 15, 1966: Signed by the New York Yankees as an amateur free agent.

November 27, 1972: Traded by the New York Yankees with Jerry Kenney, Charlie Spikes and Rusty Torres to the Cleveland Indians for Jerry Moses and Graig Nettles.

December 9, 1975: Traded by the Cleveland Indians to the Texas Rangers for Ron Pruitt and Stan Thomas.

March 30, 1982: Released by the Texas Rangers.

Courtesy Baseball Reference

How to Apply For Assistance

Oncology social workers at the foundation's partnering Connecticut hospitals and cancer centers assist cancer patients being treated at their respective facility with a simple application process.

• Cancer patient must be a Connecticut resident and in active treatment for cancer.

• Application must be accompanied by a letter of support from an Oncology Social Worker verifying patient diagnosis and financial need.

• Applications for assistance are reviewed and carefully considered by the CCF Executive Director.

• Each request is evaluated based on pre-established criteria and guidelines including patient need and availability of funds.

• Except in unusual circumstances, grants are awarded directly to the patient.

• Once a completed application and necessary documentation is received, a grant is often delivered within days.

• Yale/Smilow Cancer Center patients must apply directly to the Social Work Department at Smilow.

• Hartford Hospital patients must apply directly to the Social Work Department at Hartford Hospital.

• L+M Hospital patients must apply directly to the Social Work Department at L+M Hospital.

• Harold Leever Regional Cancer Center patients must apply directly to the Social Work Department at HLRCC.

Acknowledgments

Many thanks to:

Veteran journalist, my wife, Jacqueline R. Smith for copy editing the book and for her encouragement and guidance. My long-time editor at The Hartford Courant and The Day of New London Reid MacCluggage for his advice on this story. My daughter and journalist Stephanie Susan Smith who read portions and provided good feedback and support. Carol Nobles Bauman for reading this tale and for her suggestions on making it better.

For access to their photo and story files: Executive Editor Tim Cotter and sportswriter Vickie Fulkerson of The Day of New London; former Executive Editor James Conrad of the Norwich Bulletin; Editor and Publisher Andrew Julien of The Hartford Courant, especially for the late Courant sports columnists Bill Lee and Bob Sudyk.

Diane Pontious took most of the photos at foundation events.

Erika Ellis, John Ellis Jr., Dave Ellis, Dan Adams, Brittney Blye, Marilyn Malerba, Joe Stellato, Maynard Strickland, Roy White, Eliot White, Joachim Yahalom, for their insights on Jane, John and the foundation. The staff of the Connecticut State Library, especially Reference Librarian Susan Bigelow, for working above and beyond the call of duty in this age of Covid-19, in helping to research this book through their newspaper microfilm files. New London City Clerk Jonathan Ayala for his assistance researching land records.

Patrick Henri and Rich Marazzi of Ansonia for, among other things, insights into John's father Louis. To the late Louis Ellis for his incredible scrapbook of his son's career, given to John only upon his father's death.